THE PROMISE OF DESPAIR

More titles in the Living Theology series

A Community Called Atonement
Scot McKnight

Nature's Witness: How Evolution Can Inspire Faith
Daniel M. Harrell

Manifold Witness: The Plurality of Truth
John R. Franke

emergent
village

Connect and keep talking at
the Emergent Village website
(www.emergentvillage.com)

THE WAY
OF THE
CROSS
AS
THE WAY
OF THE
CHURCH

THE PROMISE OF DESPAIR

ANDREW ROOT

ABINGDON PRESS / Nashville

THE PROMISE OF DESPAIR
THE WAY OF THE CROSS AS THE WAY OF THE CHURCH

Copyright © 2010 by Abingdon Press

Library of Congress Cataloging-in-Publication Data

Root, Andrew, 1974-
   The promise of despair : the way of the Cross as the way of the church / Andrew Root.
      p. cm. — (Living theology series ; 4)
   Includes bibliographical references and index.
   ISBN 978-1-4267-0062-0 (trade pbk. : alk. paper)
   1. Mission of the church. 2. Despair—Religious aspects—Christianity. I. Title.
   BV601.8.R66 2010
   262'.7--dc22

                                                                    2009048171

10 11 12 13 14 15 16 17 18 19—10 9 8 7 6 5 4 3 2 1

MANUFACTURED IN THE UNITED STATES OF AMERICA

To two four-year-olds
Benjamin Oliver (1975–1979),
my first friend

and

Owen Andrew Root,
who opens his heart to me,
and whose thoughts and ideas open up the
universe—it is where I desire to live

CONTENTS

CONTENTS

INTRODUCTION TO LIVING THEOLOGY
Tony Jones, Series Editor

I know a lot of theologians, and I don't know one who wants to hide theology under a bushel. No, they want to let it shine. But far too often, the best theology is hidden under a bushel of academic jargon and myriad footnotes. Such is the life of many a professor.

But in Emergent Village, we've always wanted to talk about the best theology around, and to do it in ways that are approachable for many people. Therefore, it makes a lot of sense for us to partner with our friends at Abingdon Press to produce a series of books of approachable theology—of "living theology."

Our friends who are writing in this series have academic chops: they can write the 400-page monograph with 800 footnotes. But that's not what we've asked them to do. Instead, we've asked them to write something they're passionate about, something that they think the rest of the church should be passionate about, too.

The result, we hope, is a series that will provoke conversation around ideas that matter to the Christian faith. We expect these books to be useful in church small groups and seminary classrooms and Emergent Village cohorts (our local incarnation). Likely, they'll raise as many questions as they answer.

And, in so doing, these books will not only tackle theological issues; they'll also promote a way of doing theology: one that is conversational, collegial, and winsome. Those of us who are involved in this series hold our own convictions, but we do so with enough humility to let contrary opinions shape us, too.

It's a messy endeavor, theology. But it's also fun and, in my experience, uniquely rewarding. So we offer this series to Christ's church, with a prayer that it will draw many closer to God and further down the journey of faith.

Grace and Peace.

PREFACE

M Y SON OWEN (whom you'll hear a lot about in the pages that follow) has come to the age where video games are very important to him. He recently told me that he wished real life were as fun as the PlayStation game *Star Wars Lego*. In the movie rental store he loves looking at the covers of all the games, bringing game after game to me, asking if we can get it. I always say no for a number of reasons, but mostly because he always seems to grab the games that look the most adult in their content, the ones with parental warnings stamped all over them.

This preface (and really any preface) is the parental warning to this book. It tells you, the reader, what to expect and what not to expect, hopefully keeping you from any surprises while not ruining the fun of the content inside. To that end, as you continue there are a few things you should know. First, you should be aware that this book is in many ways written for me; it is my journey to grapple with how to be Christian and how to understand the church in our time. I personally think theology is done best this way, as a way of saving our own faith. Because of that I don't shy away from placing myself (and my family) in its pages. The book calls for a Christianity and a church that honestly wrestle with the suffering of our common human existence; therefore, it only seems right to portray my own existential journey in its contents.

Second, I may have been more honest than some readers will feel comfortable with. I admit that death scares the crap out of me. I admit that though I have tried to live a hyper-positive Christianity, it has not protected me from this fear. Some readers may think that as Christians we need not worry about death, that death isn't an issue. But I contend in these pages that it is—that even in trust and hope in the good news of the gospel we still confront the reality of nothingness with fear and trembling.

Third, I should say what I mean by *death* (and this is very important). Death is the reality of dying, of someone being placed in a grave and never being seen again. I will share some of my own experiences with this. But in this book death is not only the experience of dying but also the experience of lost jobs, marriages gone cold, bills piling up, children addicted, dreams not met, loneliness suffered. In other words, if death had a Facebook profile its interests would not only be putting people in the grave but also killing their dreams, their loves, their peace, their dignity. To signal this I call death "the monster," for it not only kills but seeks to destroy—even when it doesn't stop our breathing. I understand that we have been taught not to be afraid of death, but I think this blind religious commitment may be what is wrong with the church. I believe that the Christian tradition calls us to face the monster, to seek God in the midst of all of our experiences of death, and this I believe is the way to be church in our context.

Fourth, please don't confuse this work. This is not my attempt at a book like *Tuesdays with Morrie*, that sentimental romp by Mitch Albom that seeks life lessons through the eyes of one so close to death. I'm neither old enough nor wise enough to offer you such a read. Rather, this book in many ways is an anti–*Tuesdays with Morrie*; it is a book that sees no kind, wise sentimentality in death but only a hell— a hell that drives me to seek God, to seek a church that can be real and honest enough to speak to the reality of death. I hope at some much later date, when I am on my deathbed, that I can pass on wisdom in gratitude as I face death; but to do this, I must face it now. I must be able to look the monster in the eyes and articulate how I see it roaming our world. I must seek God in the darkness of reality.

Finally, the theological argument I'll make in this book, I believe, stands within a tradition, born from the early Protestant Reformation, that has not (most especially in

America) been embraced. While the Reformation has obviously had huge ramifications in the last five hundred years, its deeply existential theology, a theology that grapples with death and seeks God in suffering, has not been as prominent. Therefore, part one is a cultural examination of how death is present today, how it seeps through the cracks, cracks that are expanding, in our late modern world. Part two seeks to pick up and reflect on the early Reformation perspective that has too often been passed over, to articulate a theology for the church born from Luther's theology of the cross that speaks to the cultural realities laid out in part one. Therefore, I argue that as the church evolves in a new cultural reality it should return (often for the first time) to the theology that gave birth to the Reformation, a theology that finds God in death and despair. This means the reader is provided not only with cultural analysis and constructive theology, but also with a particular reading of Martin Luther and his relevance for our context.

At the end of each chapter I present two elements for further thought. First, I've provided a short exposition on a biblical figure, seeing how God moves salvation history through that person's experiences of despair. You will find (mostly in the second half) biblical texts to illustrate my theological point, but I thought this short biblical exposition would be helpful to see that throughout the biblical narrative God encounters people in despair for the sake of God's promised presence. Second, I have provided some discussion questions that will take you deeper into the biblical text and the chapter to which it relates. It may be that theology is written in solitude, but it is almost always worked out with others; therefore, it is my hope that as you read this book you can meet with others and discuss it.

There have been many others with whom I have explicitly and implicitly worked on this project; I owe them a great thanks. Tim West at Abingdon Press has been a wonderful editor to work with; he has provided a number of significant suggestions that have made this book so much better. Tony Jones, the editor of the series, has been a significant friend to me for the last handful of years. It was Tony, after hearing about this thesis in the corner of Dun Brothers in St. Anthony Park, who first saw its potential. I owe so much to Tony, mostly for his graciousness to still want to be my friend after I refused to have lunch with him when we first met in the cafeteria of Princeton Seminary (something he never lets me forget—seriously, dude, I'm sorry!).

Two of my colleagues, Amy Marga and David Lose, read and provided essential feedback on the manuscript. They both are dear friends with incredibly sharp theological minds. It is a treasure to work with them. Our family friend Stephanie Ward Lacy was also kind enough to read the whole manuscript, giving feedback from the perspective of someone not trained theologically. Her comments were invaluable. Steph has endured so much in these last few years; it is both humbling and a joy for me if she finds even one sentence of this work balm for her broken heart.

If there is an intellectual father of this work, it is Douglas John Hall. First through Doug's writing and then through our friendship he has provided me frameworks for working out my own theological perspective. And while I could not have worked these thoughts out without Doug, they are my own; all of the book's shortcomings are mine. I'm so appreciative of his kindness. I only hope I can be as kind and helpful one day to another young theologian as Doug Hall has been to me.

Finally, to Kara, who keeps me grounded in her love for me and for the little church she pastors: this book is written from the fuel of your support and the substance of your vocation as a pastor. You are the best of friends and a gifted minister. And to my children, Maisy and particularly Owen (to whom this work is dedicated). You are the greatest treasures of my life; my being suffers you, for I love you both more than my being can contain.

And now to the God of the cross, who brings from death life, calling us to seek for God in what is broken so that we might be made whole, be the glory.

INTRODUCTION

I WAS FOUR YEARS OLD. I can't say I remember it like
it was yesterday or that the memories and time line are
so strong that they haunt me. But I do remember it
clearly; it is one of the earliest memories I have. And to be
honest, I think it has shaped my life more than I had ever
realized. It started with a phone call and ended (though I'm
learning the event has never left me) with me throwing my
four-year-old body on the floor. It was a Sunday morning
and we had just returned home from church. As the afternoon sunbeams flooded our little living room, the tele-
phone rang. Picking up the phone my mom said a few
words and then hung up. Turning to me, she said, "Andy, I
have to tell you something. Benjamin is dead!" All I could
do was collapse. *Dead!*

We are often told that four-year-olds can't think
abstractly, that they can't comprehend concepts like death.
But I understood. Benjamin was four himself; he had been
my best friend, my first friend. Just one house sat between
his and mine. There are pictures of us hugging, climbing an
apple tree, and playing baseball. But Benjamin had gotten
cancer and now at the ripe old age of four he was dead.
Dead! Death! Never coming back! In the ground forever!
His little being had been swallowed up and he would never
return, and my own four-year-old being was knocked to the
floor by the force of such a reality.

How can it be that a four-year-old could get cancer and
die? How can a child be lost, mauled by a dog, killed by an
allergic reaction? How can it be that a mother of three young
children could die in her bed? How can a father, son, friend,
niece be lost *forever*, sliding into the dark pit of infinite separation? And even more ordinary (but just as heavy), how can
it be that the love of a marriage can be eroded from the

inside, killing the relationship, leaving us with the feelings of death? How can miscommunication distance us, separating friends, pushing children from parents? Why is it that every failure at work, every sign that we're not meeting expectations, forces a fissure at the core of our being, fissures that seem to allow the dark waters of death to flood us?

How can it be that at any moment death could reach up and do the scariest of things: separate us—separate us from one another, from our bodies, from our love, from our purpose, from our meaning, and even from this world—separate us from all that is? It is not dying that scares me, it's separation. I tremble when I think about what the moment will be like, that moment when I am here, but then . . . bang . . . black . . . I'm gone; I'm separated from all I am and have known. And if I'm honest, I know these moments of separation already (which is why I avoid thinking about them). I know them in rejection, failure, and loss; I can taste them on my lips when I'm depressed, stressed, and anxious. Death is on its way; death is now here when a fight with my wife seems to ossify and lead to distance, when I've been laid off and told I'm no longer needed. Death surrounds us. The crazy thing is that it's not just a bad dream. I taste death now—taste even now what awaits me, something that awaits you. By the fact that I am alive my destiny is that moment, and every small and large moment of despair points to it. By the fact that I am, I'm on a collision course with that moment of dreadful nothingness, of frightening separation. How can it be that I could *soon* so suddenly no longer be? How can it be that so much happens in life that sings the song of death?

Benjamin was *gone*. These questions, already somewhere hidden inside my four-year-old being, hidden inside all of us, thrust me to the floor.

I remember my mom picking me up and holding me, and standing me on my feet; then I walked away to my room. I'm sure I was aware that my parents went to the funeral, but I didn't go. I never remember them broaching the subject again.

At four, I had seen it, I had seen its ghastly face and it had clobbered me and I was never the same. At four I looked into the eyes of death and knew it was a dark monster that has no mercy, not even for four-year-old boys who loved making mud pies. I know it touched my parents deeply; they too had looked the monster in the eyes. That's probably why they never discussed with me what I saw. They hoped, I imagine, that if they kept quiet and looked the other way the monster would pass by our house. But after watching death indiscriminately swallow little Benjamin they also knew that it could attack at any time, that it could even reach me. Years after, whenever I would tell my mom I had a weird bump somewhere, terror would race across her face and she would sprint to examine it. I imagine that's how it started with Benjamin: an odd lump, discovered during a bath, that soon grew to destroy him.

Benjamin was gone from the earth, gone from the living, and I was still here, still alive, climbing the same apple tree, watching his little sister play with mine, seeing his dad cut the grass. But he was gone and *never* coming back. I played in baseball games, had my first kiss, sneaked out of my house on warm summer nights, watched countless hours of MTV, went to college, made new friends, discovered my voice, fell in love, had children; but Benjamin—Benjamin died. He got none of it, not even riding a yellow bus to school, never feeling the soft lips of a girls on his own, never holding a child that was his own, never ripping open an envelope to discover he got accepted, that his future had taken a happy new direction.

When he was sick in the hospital, Benjamin painted me a ceramic Indian chief's head. I kept it on my wall all the years I lived in my parents' house (and still have it). Growing up I would look at it once in a while, usually in the middle of feeling rejected, confused, or lost. I would look at it and remember Benjamin; I would remember that death had taken him, and it felt like it was breathing down my neck.

MY HAPPY JESUS

On the wall that held the ceramic Indian head, I also had a picture of Jesus. It was a picture given to me at my baptism, a picture of Jesus surrounded by four children, taking them onto his lap. It was such a nice picture, welcoming, Jesus freely inviting children, looking like a beloved uncle or the ultimate kindergarten teacher. Jesus seemed so approachable, so easygoing, so tame. I still have this picture as well, and in many ways I like it. But there was something strange about the contrast between these two wall decorations. Hidden within the Indian head was a literal hell, painted by the hand of a dying child. And next to it, a sweet Jesus, handsome and cheerful in every way, like the lead character on some ABC Family Channel sitcom, taking perfect, healthy children onto his lap. This exquisite Jesus holding these children seemed to know nothing of the hell that Benjamin knew. It appeared that Jesus was for the living, not the dead; for strong and cute kids, not emaciated, bald ones like Benjamin and those he sat near as he attentively and with great care made me a gift. Jesus was for the whole, not the shattered; Jesus was for the clean and bright, not for those so beaten and bound that all they knew was darkness.

A few months after Benjamin's death I started having nightmares, terrible nightmares, nightmares that placed my name on the church prayer chain, nightmares that had words like *demonic* attached to them when the old ladies at church prayed for me. No one ever thought that just maybe my nightmares and Benjamin's death were connected. For Jesus wasn't found in the forsaken world of ceramic Indian heads, but only on the green pastures where happy and healthy children played. The power of death's ability to annihilate four-year-olds and my bad dreams seemed to have nothing to do with each other. I heard a lot of children's sermons about being a sinner and needing to be nice to my baby sister, and Jesus sure seemed nice in the pictures I colored and in the one hanging on my wall. But no one at church had anything to say about the monster that had taken my friend; Jesus seemed not to go into those dark corners in my own being that was aware (aware without words) that the monster of death could get me too.

DENNY, DEATH, AND BASEBALL

In the spring of my fifth-grade year the monster of death struck again. It was the weekend that my friends and I anticipated every year: the annual association baseball and softball tournament. The park fields were brimming with kids in assorted colored T-shirts, hauling gloves, bats, and cleats, and parents with lawn chairs and blankets. This was the weekend that all the association teams from each age group vied for elementary school immortality, where we sought to lead our teams to the title and get that big plastic trophy. It was such a great event because we not only played in our own games, but after they were finished we could take our bikes and spend hours flirting with girls, eating candy, and watching our friends play.

On this day my team had been eliminated, and I changed out of my uniform and rode my bike back up to the park to watch my friends play in the championship game. I set my bike on the ground and stood behind Denny. Denny was my neighbor and my friend's dad. He was in a wheelchair after suffering an accident many years before. Standing with us was Mr. Snyder and his oldest son. I watched the game leaning on Denny's chair with a wad of Big League chewing gum in my mouth. In the fourth inning Denny hunched over and grabbed fiercely at the chain-link fence in front of him, his head down as he mumbled something incomprehensible. Terror rushed through my body. I turned and got Mr. Snyder's attention, and as I did, everything changed. I actually felt myself sliding back as though I were being pulled out of the scene. Mr. Snyder yelled, "Denny! Denny, what's wrong? Someone get some help!" And I just stood there shocked, afraid. One of the managers of the association ran to the warming house to reach the phone. I can still see the panic in his face as his middle-aged body raced across the green grass.

I stood there shocked, feeling invisible and overburdened by the situation I was watching. But I wasn't the only one watching. Jared, Denny's son, was just feet away from his dad, bat in hand and batting helmet on his head, standing on deck; he too was sucked back from the chaos, fear painted all over his face. The field seemed to darken. It could have been dusk setting in, the regular storm system of a late May afternoon in the Midwest, or just how I remember it. The ambulance arrived. They strapped Denny to the gurney and took him away, rushing him to the hospital, but he was already gone. A brain aneurism and he was gone, and Jared was up next to bat as the ambulance sped away. They continued the game, Jared stepping into the batter's box and striking out. After the game I rode my bike home alone, scared, racing as fast as I could as though death were chasing me through the paths that wound through the perfectly manicured lawns of my suburban neighborhood. I chose not to tell anyone, not even my parents; I was too afraid, my being still shaken from Benjamin. The monster had attacked again, death was coming for me, separation was inevitable. I was scared, so scared that I became scared forevermore.

A SCARED JESUS LOVER

Then I became "that kid"—the junior higher and senior higher who is the model confirmation student, the model youth group participant. I said long prayers, believed my prayers, and told people about Jesus. I was that kid who went to all the parties but never drank; I was that kid (I squirm as I write this) who did signs of religious devotion on the varsity baseball field and the hockey rink. I was described as "on fire" for my faith and I had the music, T-shirts, and books to prove it. But I wasn't on fire, I was scared. Scared of striking out, scared of looking foolish, scared of being rejected, scared of . . . I'm not sure what, I was just scared. We're all scared, but for me these things all felt so important, so heavy, so frightening, so dreadful that I needed help. I needed Jesus to protect me from them, to give me success, to be a bubble that could insulate me from all that threatened me, from the monster of death and its ability to separate, which I knew was always lurking. Maybe we all feel like I did or maybe fear weighed so heavily on me because of Benjamin and then Denny, because I had seen death and it had thrown my being to the floor. I had tasted it and knew, even at four, that I was next— maybe not tomorrow, but someday. I had looked into the void and every time it showed itself my being was sent back to the trauma of when it first appeared, suffocating Benjamin's being. Every strikeout, bad date, doubt of my future, and so much more reminded me that I was next, that I was in danger, that death was going to get me and even now in a small way was having its way with me. I was so scared of this reality that I needed Jesus and all his bad music, T-shirts, and youth group events to remind me that I was OK, that I was special, that I was safe because I could pray or quote a Bible verse. I had power when I felt so small, and Jesus gave it to me. Jesus was in my heart, keeping me safe. Benjamin was dead, but I had Jesus!

But there was something else that Benjamin's death did to me. It forced me to think. Experiencing death so up close and alone, with no cultural rituals or communication with adults but having to bear it alone by my four-year-old self, made me think. As a fifth grader on my BMX bike, trying to outrace death's ominous lurching, again I was forced to think. I was forced to be reflective. I was forced in an odd way to be honest. Death is in the world: it eats four-year-olds, it strikes fathers as they watch their sons play baseball, it weasels its way between loved ones, it steals people's identity and meaning, it can't be ignored. I was scared but I was also forced to be honest—honest at least about my vulnerability, which I guess is what made me so scared to begin with.

Upon graduation I decided to spend my college years at a nice, small, conservative, evangelical institution. It was what was best for me at the time (though I now regret how much money it cost). But living away from my parents and surrounded with other scared Jesus lovers like myself, I found truth and honesty spilling from my pores. I don't mean that pompously, as though I possessed the truth. I simply found myself saying things, crass (and funny) things that everyone else was thinking but was too afraid to say. In the arms race to be more and more holy I was struck by the absurdity it of it all. The contest to out-pray, out-integrity, and out-serve your classmates to show that you were a mature Christian led me back to Benjamin and back to the day in the park. Benjamin was dead, I was next, and all I could say about Jesus was that he wanted me to pray more, raise my hands when I worshiped, and find the perfect Christian girl. This all seemed absurd. My faith, after so many years, had nothing to say to Benjamin, nothing to say to Denny, nothing to say to the deep questions surrounding my being that Denny and Benjamin's deaths brought to the surface.

A NEW VISION

It was right there in black and white, right there in the required reading for a seminary class, right there for my eyes to read over and over again. "This love of God for the world does not withdraw from reality into noble souls detached from the world, but experiences and suffers the reality of the world at its worst. The world exhausts its rage on the body of Jesus Christ."[1] I kept reading it and reading it. I could almost see through the page, through the words to something different. The words seemed to penetrate my being, taking company next to those spots rubbed raw within me since Benjamin and Denny's negation, those spots that so vigorously pushed me to run from failure and fear, to not stop and admit my brokenness and yearning.

The quote came from Dietrich Bonhoeffer, the Lutheran theologian and martyr who had been killed by the Nazis for entering a conspiracy to assassinate Hitler. The quote itself apprehended me, but the fact that it was from Bonhoeffer, a pacifist pastor who chose to become a double agent, kept me entranced. Here I was presented with a Jesus who was found not in pastures of noble perfection, which my classmates in college and I had been chasing. Here was something quite different: a Jesus who was found first not in prayers and moral perfection, but in death, in suffering, on the cross. A Jesus found first embracing emaciated four-year-olds attentively painting ceramic Indian heads. I could hear new words whispered to my being. Once I had heard only, "Run, you motherf***er, you're next!" from the monster of death, forcing me into the arms of clear, safe, pretend Jesus, who in the end had no words to give my brokenness, doubts, and fright. This Jesus could only provide me an illusion, a fantasy that had little to do with a reality where death strangles us. Instead, I heard a different Jesus, a Jesus on a cross, not as a symbol but as an actuality, not as his job, but as the state of his being. I heard him saying, "Stop, turn and look; it is me, beaten, and suffering. Look! It is me, Jesus the Christ, dropping myself into the dark pit that is taking Benjamin, plunging into the storm that overcame Denny. You want me? Find me here! In the empty place of God-forsakenness, in the place where four-year-olds disappear, in the place where fathers die while their children wait on deck, it is here that I am at work. Seek me here!"

THE CHURCH AND THE FACING OF DESPAIR

In the last handful of years there have been a number of interesting (and some helpful) calls for the recasting of the Christian faith and the ministry of the church in our world. In the light of cultural transitions we have seen a need to move into new ways of thinking and doing church, new ways to speak and act with an emerging generation. These (mostly) prophetic practitioners have pleaded for the church to pull itself out of 1962 and its stilted bureaucratic forms of ministry to enter a much different world. This has been more than needed. Yet I still wonder if any of them, in their recasting, have anything to say to Benjamin and Denny, have anything to say to our world that knows death and nothingness so well in broken relationships and broken dreams. I wonder if any of them have made the place of emptiness the place of God's inbreaking, seeking to discover what this would mean for how we do church.

My family attended a small church in the uptown area of Minneapolis, a hip city neighborhood inhabited mostly by young adults. The church's building is large, and there was a time that its members filled the sanctuary to overflowing. But those days are long gone as mainline decline has wrapped itself around the congregation, shrinking it to a handful of old members and their children filling only the first few pews of the expansive sanctuary. The problem with the congregation wasn't that it was small, and not really even that it was dying. The problem with the church was that it kept acting like it was neither. Our Easter service one year summed it up. There were thirty people in the pews, twenty-five in the choir loft (including the brass section), and three fully robed (including the seminary intern) pastors. We sang a number of hymns from *The Hymnal of 1982* (that's the actual title!), listened to a moralistic sermon about triumphalism, read a prayer of confession oddly representing a rigid substitutionary atonement, and watched as all the children (there were only six of them) received their first Bibles in an act soaked in the language of civic religion. That was it. That was Easter! And I sat in my own pew and thought of Benjamin and Denny.

As I thought, I found myself focusing on the lilies and mums in the chancel and on the altar; there were more than twenty of them, all beautifully placed. I picked up my bulletin to page to the next hymn that I would daydream through, and I found myself on the last page. It read, "The lilies and mums in the sanctuary are given. . . . " Below this was written, "In memory of my parents," "In memory of Lee," "In memory of my sister," "In memory of my beloved wife." These flowers witnessed to separation, each of these flowers represented a person lost to the monster, swallowed by death. As I read I looked around the sanctuary and realized how many more lilies and mums could be placed on the altar—lilies and mums given in memory of jobs and income lost, lilies and mums given in memory of children now addicted, of relationships lost and dreams now shattered. Lillies and mums could fill the chancel and push out into the pews and aisles and spill out the windows and doorways into the street below.

These flowers, consciously placed here on Easter, represented the longing of loved ones to be reunited with those lost to death, those never coming back, those separated from all that is. Here in this dying church, in love and yearning these people had placed a flower on the altar out of despair, out of the hope that somehow the reality of Easter might touch this despair and bring life out of death. But no one said a thing about the lilies and mums. We were too busy giving out Bibles and talking about who still had their first Bibles, too busy singing in Latin, to recognize that this Sunday, at least, we celebrate an absurd truth: that death has been overcome, that God meets us in our despair and promises us life and wholeness out of death and destruction. But we just kept singing from *The Hymnal of 1982*.

And I am sure that around town in one of the many emergent or new paradigm churches there were other things going on, things I would much rather have been part of than singing from *The Hymnal of 1982*. But I wonder if they took into account Benjamin, Denny, and all those represented by lilies and mums. These new churches are considering our cultural transition, but have they thought about our despair? I know they are hipper and more interesting, but do they bleed? Are they able (brave enough) to go into that dark pit that swallows four-year-olds and fathers and do the impossible, proclaim the presence and activity of God there? Are any of our churches doing this?

AN ELEMENT FORGOTTEN: A BLEEDING CHURCH

Whenever someone critiques the prophetic practitioners on their desire to recast the Christian faith and ministry for what they usually call "a postmodern world," these critics often assert that they too easily embrace "a nihilistic postmodernism," a derogatory term they see as antithetical to classical Christianity.[2] They add nihilism to postmodernism to communicate its bankrupt-ness. In response, the prophetic practitioners (by which I mean people like Brian McLaren, Dan Kimball, and Rob Bell) have tried to defend their starting point, tried to make the case that postmodernism is not nihilistic or radically against absolute truth or whatever. *This book will agree with the critics.* I will assert that the critics are right that there is something nihilistic, something about nothingness and bankrupt-ness, in the transitions of our context, something maybe even against classic Christianity, by which of course the critics mean Christianity as the dominate cultural religion. But unlike the fearmongering of the critics and the defensive stance of the prophetic practitioners, I seek to embrace this nihilism. I want to assert, "You're right. Our context is filled with nihilism, as is my being, with the hopelessness of death, with the fear of separation, with the impossibility that no one can save fathers from brain aneurysms or four-year-olds from cancer. You're right. There is little in our context that is real enough to allow us somewhere to belong." But instead of starting with a critique and nostalgic wishes of a time before nihilism came into view, or trying to defend our revitalization from being seen as nihilistic, what if we simply started here? What if we sought God in the nothingness, in the kenosis, in the emptiness that the Philippians hymn tells us Jesus takes on? What if this is the most faithful way to be the people of God?

We have talked so much about the need to do church differently, about the need to think about our faith differently. But have we actually taken the time to construct our ministerial action around a God who meets us in the death of the cross, a God who gives Godself over to annihilation? Have we recognized that Christian people, people who follow Jesus, are weird people? We are people who worship a God become human who dies, who not only dies but is crucified.

I know we have been taught to be positive, that we have been told that our Christianity will keep us happy and hopeful (and, as I will argue later, there is something in Christian faith that moves into joy, thanksgiving, and rich hope). But too often we have been told that as Christians we need not fear death. These are words more for Hallmark cards than for reality; these are more the words of sentimentality than the words of Jesus crucified and dying. The Christian faith is a faith that has as its central event the cross, the reality of death. But this central reality is rarely the center of the church's being and action. We are a people who know and therefore confess of a time when God died, when the dark pit that destroyed Benjamin and Denny annihilated God as well. The power of Easter is that out of this utter God-forsakenness, out of this place where four-year-olds die, God rises; God is fully God, overcoming the darkness by taking it into Godself. It is into suffering (the suffering of death, nothingness, separation), the suffering of the world, taken on in the suffering of God, that the church is called.

LUTHER: A THEOLOGY OF THE CROSS FOR THE CHURCH

Before you think I'm nuts (or just really pessimistic), let me point out that these thoughts are the very theological breakthrough that brought about the Reformation. It was Martin Luther who stumbled across these ideas in his reading of Paul, in light of a church literally selling safety to scared people living in a dangerous world, surrounded by the monster of death (think of, for instance, the plague). It was Luther who shouted for the people to realize that the God made known in Jesus Christ was God found first and foremost beaten on a cross. God was first seen not in gold, not in riches and strength, not in the lovely words of most of our praise songs, but in the weakness of a beaten peasant dying alone and abandoned outside the city. We worship a crucified God, Luther asserted.

The theological breakthrough of the Reformation is the *theologia crucis*, the theology of the cross. What this book offers is a recasting of Christian faith and ministry in our time through the lens of the theology of the cross, through the confession that God meets us first in despair. Luther stated in the Heidelberg Disputation, "It is certain that [people] must utterly *despair* of [their] own ability before [they are] prepared to receive the grace of Christ."[3] For Luther this is true because God can be found first on a cross, bearing the terror of the death of four-year-olds, fathers, and lost lovers forever separated. This book, like others, seeks to recast the Christian faith in our time; but unlike them it does so by returning to the very theological perspective that bore the Reformation, the *theologia crucis*, the death of God. This book seeks a reimagining of Luther's theology of the cross for a church in late modernity. The theological argument of this book seeks a return to radical and messy theology that spawned the Reformation, a theological perspective often minimized or ignored.

But we will not do this while keeping our feet squarely in our time, in late modernity, postmodernity, a globalized world, hypermodernity, or whatever term floats your boat. Therefore, I will articulate how despair is present in our context (Part One) and how the church's call is not to solve, fix, or oppose this despair, but to enter it, to make the church's life there, to discover the promise of God within the emptiness, separation, and nihilism that we all know so well but are often too scared to admit (Part Two).

After the Roman emperor Constantine made Christianity the religion of the West in A.D. 313, the theology of the cross has been continually placed on the back pages of theological discussion. Why, after all, would a ruler in control of a state church want to emphasize that Jesus rules through weakness, death, and despair? Why would politicians seeking a bigger defense budget invoke a God made known in the absurdity of separation, death, and annihilation—in the power of the weakness of self-giving love in death? After Luther the recovery of *theologia crucis* also was underemphasized as modernity and the ideology of progress led us to believe we were moving to a better and better world.

But now, standing at the end of modernity, we know better. We know that suffering in the world is not decreasing, but increasing. We understand that the emptiness within each of us is not being filled by culture, religion, or more and more consumer goods. We are starting to realize that there is not much here at all, just images and products. Everything seems to be an illusion. There are so few things in our world to make meaning with and belong to that are more stable than individual taste, preference, or style.

PART ONE

WHEN THE MONSTER STRUCK I was four. He was five. The oldest of three children of a Lutheran pastor, he adored his father, and his father showered him with love. But by the time he was five his witty and attentive father was overcome by headaches. Soon they became debilitating, and his once loving and present father changed before his eyes, from active and strong to comatose and frail. And not long after, he was gone, dead. Lost, leaving a little boy without his hero. By the end of the year the monster would strike again, this time taking his little brother. With father and brother gone, he and his family moved to be near relatives. But only a few years later his beloved grandmother and then, soon after, his aunt were taken.

By thirteen I was scared to death, having bad dreams. By thirteen he too was having bad dreams, but his came with migraines that would punch him to the floor and force him into bed for days. Early on, these headaches would occur after he heard of someone's death. Later they would happen in the midst of disappointment and critique. Whenever the monster showed itself, pulling people into the shadows or whispering threats of destruction through rejection, depression, or humiliation, his head would feel as if it were going to implode.

I ran to a clean, pure, and pristine Jesus that could keep me safe. Braver than I, he wanted no such Jesus, no such false

Jesus who exists as a teddy bear to hide us from all that is menacing in the world. He knew that a teddy bear is not much help against a bloodthirsty monster. So he began looking for somewhere to stand more solid than my pretend Jesus, somewhere to stand safely in a world where the monster roars uncaged, picking its next victim with no discretion. He soon discovered that he had nowhere to stand, nowhere at all. He was alone; we all were alone. The Christian faith couldn't help, at least not the way it was being practiced in the European Protestant churches. Science and progress couldn't help, for just like the churches they denied the monster more than faced it. Society and country couldn't help either, for just as the church denied the monster by offering people rose-colored glasses of a future salvation, and science the placebo of progress, society and country desired to keep folks busy with things like service and patriotism—so busy that they wouldn't acknowledge the monster rambling through our neighborhoods taking children, parents, and loved ones. So busy that they wouldn't realize that our lives are frail and recognize for what it was the illusion that the nation could protect us.

This heartbroken boy, now a man, continued to seek a place to stand, searching to find such a place while overcome in his adult life by headaches, anxiety, mental breakdowns, and lonely isolation. Unlike many, he looked deeply into the eyes of the monster and saw that it takes everything. In the midst of his own struggle with the monster he uttered prophetic words that have yet to leave us. He asserted that no religion, technology, or society could overcome the emptiness that the monster leaves after it has done its deed. This five-year-old boy who lost his beloved pastor father was Friedrich Nietzsche.

NIETZSCHE

I remember clearly my first encounter with the name Nietzsche. I was in high school and visiting a contemporary worship service. After singing a few repetitive choruses the pastor came forward to welcome people. He decided to use some humor, I suppose to communicate how contemporary this service was. He said, "I was in the bathroom and I saw written on the wall 'God is dead,' and under it was scribbled 'by Friedrich Nietzsche,' but above that something else was written; it said, 'Nietzsche is dead.' " And then pausing to deliver the punch line he said, "by . . . God." Everyone laughed. I wasn't sure why. I figured the humor was in the fact that we know objectively that Nietzsche is dead—we have historical verification—but the jury is still out about God. I didn't find that funny!

Nietzsche has received a great amount of flak from church people for his so-called atheistic statements about the death of God. And it is true that Nietzsche had many hard feelings about Christianity and the church, though his mother never stopped hoping he would become a pastor like his father and grandfather. But ultimately Nietzsche's words are directed not so much toward God as they are toward us. They are not so much theological proclamations as they are philosophical statements about how we humans live and the situation we find ourselves in.

Nietzsche was not angry at Jesus but at the church. He was not asserting the failure of following Jesus Christ but the failure of Christianity as a religion and even as an institutional structure. "God is dead" is not a prescription, not even his hope; "God is dead" is his interpretation not of God but of our way of life. Looking at our world Nietzsche saw from his late nineteenth-century location that we no longer organize our lives around Providence as a guide to our lives; we no longer *really* hold that God is in control of our lives and society. We look to Doppler, not sacrifice, for rain. We trust institutions like the police force to protect us, not incantations to gods. The world Nietzsche saw was a modern world that could function without daily bidding for God's providence and protection. Nietzsche saw that God became a mascot, an add-on to the modern way of life.

We didn't *need* God; we had moved past needing God; God was dead to us, except possibly on Sundays. We didn't *need* God the way ancient people did; we had medicines, machines, and organization.

But Nietzsche saw something else that it took the rest of us a hundred years to catch on to. We essentially killed God by making God a footnote to our lives, but our new god of progress and advancement was no god worth serving. Nietzsche knew that we could deny it, but the monster still roamed, and our progress couldn't solve the issue of finitude. Nietzsche knew that this so-called modern life had more than a few holes in it. "God is dead" because we (not Nietzsche) killed God. And our modern world of progress could not replace God. We lived without God, but this modern world could not solve the problem of the monster of death. It could provide technologies to avoid it, and in our own time, shiny things to distract from it, but the world could *not* deliver us from its vicious desire to separate us from love and life. This modern way of living promised that it could, that through progress it could solve all human problems, transforming the threatening monster into a harmless puppy. But Nietzsche knew better from the beginning.

And this is why Nietzsche hated Christianity. For what Christianity did (does) in this modern world is hide or distract people from the reality of the monster and the emptiness it creates by using hollow sentimentality. It gives people easily digestible messages to keep them from ever facing reality—a reality where God is dead and we are exposed to the monster.

REPLACING PROVIDENCE WITH PROGRESS

Nietzsche saw clearly that by placing progress in the place of providence, the modern world has killed God. What happens when we realize that this so-called progress is only a lie, that it cannot provide what it promises and what we so desperately need? The monster lives; death is in the world. It takes beloved fathers, brothers, grandparents, aunts, and friends. In a world based on providence we were promised protection in the all-encompassing social reality of the local religion. In a world of progress we were promised that the monster could be eliminated. Disease, accidents, and war could be ended; the monster of death could be gutted of all its power, disappearing or becoming nothing but a puppy nipping at our heels.

But Nietzsche saw that modernity and its fetish for progress was no match for the monster. The monster of death was too massive, too cunning, too tacitly locked within us to be banished. And now what? he wondered. We have killed God, and in turn we have put institutions and machines in God's place. We have killed God and in God's place given people sentimental religious visions of a salvation that can be had without any account of the monster. If God is dead and modernity is a lie, if we have outgrown providence but cannot trust progress, then what, if anything, do we stand on?

Nietzsche's genius was that he asked these very questions generations before the rest of us could glimpse the fullness of his questions' prophetic utterance. Nietzsche saw only the triumph of the monster and its ability to strike anything into nothingness. It would not be long, he believed, until the nothingness the monster brings could decay modernity from the inside out. In mindless sentimentality we could continue to imagine we were progressing, safe from the monster, thanks to happy Christianity, but the very surface we lived on was revealing that it was not solid ground. Not only was it *not* solid ground, there was nothing much there at all. With God dead and progress a lie, there was . . . nothing!

THE LOSS OF SOLID GROUND: FROM PROGRESS TO ESCAPE

By killing God and worshiping progress we allowed the monster, death and its ability to cast people into nothingness, to be the hidden operative reality. World wars, genocides, nuclear bombs, terrorism, and global poverty would only affirm this reality of nothingness splitting the seams of modernity. And when these seams are burst, nothingness takes the place of progress. With God dead and progress a lie we realize that we are unanchored; we have fallen through the illusion of the thick crust of progress to now be swimming in a sea of doubt, a sea where little feels solid at all. Knowing there is no solid ground, but only a sea that soaks us in doubt, we have moved from progress to individual escape. We may be vulnerably bobbing in the sea of doubt, never knowing when the monster will rush to the surface to devour us; we may be floating precariously, but we can distract ourselves with products, ads, websites, and screens. We may be drowning in a vast dark sea of nothingness, but we can pretend it is only a hot tub—that we aren't vulnerable, only on vacation.

We continue to deny the monster by keeping our attention on our multiple screens, living our lives through electronic platforms. Staring at flat HD screens, iPhones, and Facebook profiles, we seek to construct some meaning for ourselves now that the monster has had victory over simple religion and modern progress. We consume new things, things that give us identity in a world where meaning has been hollowed out by the nothingness that death breathes upon it. New shoes and new cars seem to give us at least something by which to define ourselves, something to be as we bob in the sea of nothingness all around us, since religion and progress are now unable to give us any definition of who we are and why we are alive. And of course once this new "stuff" has lost its newness it has lost its buoyancy, and we must swim to something else for escape or drown.

Nietzsche knew that once God is dead and the inventions of modernity are shown to be more pathetic than genius, then we are faced with a void of authority. The progress of modernity pushes God from the center and places itself (with its science and technology) on the throne as the new king. But the rule under modernity's *coup d'etat* has been anything but utopian. When it is realized that science, technology, and bureaucracy secretly serve the monster to keep their power (as the twentieth century has shown they do), they can no longer be trusted. But what can be trusted? What is the answer to the question *Says who?* We have decided that in the end it is only I; nothing beyond the individual has authority.

At first glance this too seems ingenious. Yet, the problem is that once authority is determined solely by me I realize I am alone. I realize that I have lost belonging or must formulate relationships in new, much riskier ways that make my belonging always tenuous, for there is nothing that binds us other than our choice. So while I am free, I am alone; my relationships and communities become episodic, often disappearing into the void of nothingness that the monster wants for me. I find myself separated more than connected, nearer to death than to life.

Though we may want to deny it (especially those of us in the church, which is quite a shame), death and its promise of nothingness is closer to us than ever. With God dead and modernity's promises shown to be a lie, we are exposed. Neither religion nor progress can save us! We are laid bare to the monster not just at the end of our lives or in the sudden puncture of our lives by tragedy; the monster, death and suffering, runs through the fabric of our American culture. Nothingness is ever close to us overexposed late (post) modern people. We confront death not just in funerals or accident scenes but also in our malls, living rooms, boardrooms, and bus stops. We confront it in the mundane and the regular, for the sunblock of religion and progress has been wiped off of our collective consciousness. We are clawing for something real to hold on to as nothingness surrounds us. We have no answer for its nearness, nor hope that it can be overcome; we have only distractions, simulations, and consumptions to keep us from being paralyzed. But death is here. It is right here; it is peering at you even now, looking over your shoulder as you read. The nothing-ness wrapped around our world plays a song that when you are quiet you can hear in the rattles of our culture; but to your shock you can also hear your own being morosely whistling along.

As this book unfolds we will see the great paradox of the gospel: that we can only overcome death by entering it. Not by denying it, whether through more religion or more mod-ern (postmodern) forms of doing church. We will see if such reflection might not help us think about how to do ministry in this context where nothingness surrounds us, where despair is so close.[1] But before we can go here, we need to push my assertions further, seeing how death and nothing-ness is running through the streams of culture.

CHAPTER ONE

DISNEYLAND AND THE DEFECATING GOAT

The Death of Meaning

I HAD A REALIZATION NOT LONG AGO, a realization that I was already aware of (by definition that may keep it from being a realization, but bear with me). I had never thought too much about this, but it became clear to me in the middle of February that nearly all of my waking hours were spent in one of two places. Not two buildings, like home and work, but literally two places, two three-foot by five-foot areas. Almost all of my other movements were either en route to these two places or excursions that frustrated me from being at one or the other of these places. In the middle of a cold Minnesota winter I realized that most of my time was spent either sitting in a chair looking at my computer or lying on my living room floor watching TV. I had a whole house with multiple rooms, but all I really did was lie in one spot staring at one corner night after night, hour after hour. I began to wonder why I had these other rooms (especially the ones without a TV). I had a whole office, but most of the time I was in it I was popping in and out of windows that took me to other places, pushing a piece of plastic around my desk to take me in and out of these worlds. Almost all of my life in these winter months was framed by a screen. I was alive, living a very short life, but most of my attention was bound within thirty-six or thirteen inches.

SCREEN LIVING

And of course this screen living is not just for workaholics and homebodies like me. Even those always on the go, young adults and business people, bring their screens with them, using their screens to distract them from the mundane flow of life, or as an eye to see their world (hence the explosion of YouTube). This point was driven home one night, yes, as I was lying on my living room floor watching TV. On the late night talk show *Jimmy Kimmel Live*, Kanye West was performing. When he was introduced and began his performance the camera zoomed in tightly on him, but as he continued, it panned out, showing the audience. As it did I could see the first dozen or so rows, and in them were hundreds of cell phone cameras being held up. These young people had chosen to watch (and record) Kanye's performance through their personal two-inch screens. On my screen, I watched them watch Kanye on theirs. Physically at the concert, they chose nevertheless to take in the experience through their screens.

Now don't get me wrong. I'm no TV hater. If I could find a way to watch while I slept, I might. And every ideological TV hater I've ever known has made me suspicious. We once lived in an apartment building with one of these folks. She was always bragging about how she didn't watch TV, ranting about its banality. Once, she walked through our apartment, and some boring program about the interior design of the White House was on TV. She stood there staring at it for fifteen minutes like my dogs look at my dinner. Spellbound, she would break her gaze every few minutes and smile at us as if to say, "Isn't this great? Wow, this is fun." I finally had to turn the TV off to free her from its tractor beam so she could leave.

But recently I became more aware of how these screens were framing my whole life. How this displaced me and connected me. How I was participating in the lives of these characters I watched, or more accurately, how they were participating in mine. I felt somehow oddly connected to the kids on *The Hills* (and my wife felt so connected that she become enraged with cocky, chauvinistic Spencer, wishing she could kick him right in the you-know-what).

I only knew the characters through this screen, and they had no idea who I was, but they were having an effect on my life. I was attentively watching them, enjoying them, living alongside them. I could feel my being soaking in the stories and characters of the shows I watched. But none of them were real! They're prepared realities, created in sound stages. They're not "real," just simulations of real life. Even so-called reality TV isn't "real." There may be people using their real names, but what we see on the screen is prepared through editing, cameras, and the structure of the show (for example, you have to follow the rules of the game to be on *Survivor*).

I was living a real life, aware, if I would stop and listen, that it was finite and could end at any moment. We know life's realness when we think of the fragility of our loves and jobs. My life was real, but I was spending my whole winter watching unreal things, and not just watching but entering into them, taking them into my being, using them to make meaning. I was using these images on the screen as brick and mortar to create a meaningful place in which to live. The screen feigned solid brick and bonding mortar, but they had been hollowed out; they were only translucent images, in the end not real enough to build a structure of meaning from. I was using unreal things to make meaning. It wasn't the story of my ancestors or the perspectives of the church community or the views of my neighbors that I was using as raw material to construct meaning (what it meant to be living), it was Michael from *The Office*, Locke from *Lost*, and all those warped kids from *The Real World*.

My wife is part of a neighborhood baby group. It is a group of mostly mothers with small children that meets every week to allow the children to play and the mothers to commune over coffee. As they talked while breaking up toddler conflicts one week, one of the moms said, "Oh! Something embarrassing happened to me this week! I was talking with a coworker who said something that reminded me of something that happened to one of my friends. I couldn't remember which friend, but I vividly remembered the situation, so I began telling my coworker about the incident, 'Yeah, something like that happened to one of my friends . . .' About halfway through the story I realized to my shock that I was relaying a plot from a rerun of *Friends*." Everyone laughed heartily at the embarrassment of the situation but I imagine also at the fact that it could have been any of them.

JEAN BAUDRILLARD

The French philosopher and social theorist Jean Baudrillard spilled a good amount of ink making many of these very points. Baudrillard wondered whether, in our screen-based worlds, we have lost the ability to construct meaning. He wondered whether meaning had died, drowned in a tidal wave of images.

Baudrillard asserted that meaning, especially meaning formed through language, is constructed through a structure of signs and things the signs signify. For instance, my one-year-old daughter is learning to talk. Her favorite word (besides *Mama*) is *daaga* (translated *dog*). She learned to speak the sign, daaga, because of her delight with these two huge, furry, four-legged things that walked around her, licking her face, and allowing her to grab them. At first, when she would see them she would simply scream with glee, but soon she learned the sign to signify them. With her first, daaga, she was connecting the sign (daaga) with the thing it signified (four-legged, furry thing that licks my face). The sign is not the thing; it is only a signifier, a pointer, daaga, a label for the thing itself. Now that she can connect the sign (daaga) with the thing it signifies (four-legged, furry animal), with great pride she uses the sign all the time. Seeing a dog blocks away she points and shouts, "Daaga, daaga." She is making meaning, using the structure to organize and make sense of her world.

Images in their own way are signs; they point to or reflect something real, the signified, helping us make sense and meaning out of our worlds. Eating a delicious chocolate chip cookie at our corner bakery I see a sign with an image of a glass of milk. My mouth waters not for the sign—I don't feel the urge to rip the poster off the wall and start licking it—rather, the sign, the image of the glass of milk, gives me the urge to go to the counter to purchase a real glass of milk. I return to my table to finish my cookie, now ignoring the sign. It has done its job; it pointed me to that which it signified, to the cold, wet glass of milk in my hand. I used the sign to make meaning out of my urge and need. I used the sign to be led into an encounter with the signified, with the glass of milk itself.

What Baudrillard argues is that in our time of screen living we have become bombarded with signs, and in the midst of the bombardment the sign has become dislocated from the thing it signifies. The sign has become so inflated that it has outgrown the thing it signifies; the sign no longer serves the thing itself but has dethroned it. Advertising for a product is no longer concerned with how it works (it is better, brighter, clearer, faster) but with what it means, what it means to put on the sign of Nike or Apple. It is about the sign alone. It is not about what the shoe does, for instance; rather, it is about the sign the shoe presents. It doesn't necessarily matter whether the product works; what matters is what it means to put on its sign. This makes meaning quite thin, for it stands on little that is solid; the sign, the image, has become all that there is. Signs disconnected from their signifier are what we are using to make meaning. Signs, images, are no longer pointers, paths to the signified; in our screen world they are the destination.

SIMULATION AS LIFE

Baudrillard believes simulation has become life itself. We are making meaning not with real things but with simulated realities (like models, celebrities, and web pages). Instead of simulation representing something more real than itself, in our image-based screen world simulation no longer follows the real thing but goes ahead of it. The simulation has lost its trail of breadcrumbs back to the original. We peer at simulations of life to tell us how to live our real lives. When pastors get prayer requests for hurt or sick soap opera characters (which has been documented to happen, and more often than you might think), the simulation has become the thing, the simulated sign has outgrown the signified life. When "reporting on the [first Gulf] war . . . the news channel CNN switches to a group of reporters 'live' . . . to ask them what was happening, only to discover that they were watching CNN to find out themselves. . . . Simulation precede[s] reality, making what is real, true, moral, and right hard to hold."[1]

We have always had simulations; from cave drawings to early maps, we have always sought to represent real life through simulated means. But in our world framed by screens, we run the danger of our maps becoming more captivating than the location itself. Some people feel more themselves—more real—online than off.

When my contractor sketches a plan for finishing my basement, it is clearly a simulation; I don't confuse it for the thing itself. As I begin working I see how at odds the drawing is with the actual basement. Though the wall was supposed to, according to the simulation of the drawing, go against the foundation, it has to be moved out a foot because of how the foundation was formed. What is real is not the plan but the work and constraints of the basement.

Yet in one of my favorite *South Park* episodes we see what happens when the simulation becomes the thing. In this sarcasm-laced episode Stan and Kyle are playing *Guitar*

Hero, the video game whereby using a guitar-shaped controller you can simulate being, well, a guitar hero. You don't need any guitar skills, just the ability to hit certain buttons at certain times. Stan and Kyle have become so good that the neighborhood kids have come to watch them. Hearing old 1970s and 1980s rock songs coming from the living room, Stan's dad inquires about what the boys are doing. In the next scene we see Stan's dad standing with his guitar and amp really playing the songs the boys are simulating on the video game. "See," he says, "I can really play these songs. Cool, huh? I can teach you." But they don't care about playing the real songs, they care only about the simulation. The image-based simulation has become more captivating than the real thing. They don't care that he can really play the songs; they are using the simulation as a self-enclosed world unto itself. It is no longer a simple simulation that incompletely represents the real thing; if it were, they would be drawn to Stan's dad and his real playing. But they care little about the real thing; the simulation stands on its own and has evolved beyond its link to its original. Baudrillard calls this the hyperreal.[2] We use unreal signs to inform and direct our real lives.

A further example will help. When my wife was pregnant with our son, we saw a midwife named Greta who was originally from Germany, which was evident by her accent and her direct manner of relating. One month, as my wife was in for her regular checkup, we asked Greta if she had seen the show *A Baby Story*, a half-hour show that follows a woman from the last weeks of pregnancy through labor and birth to the celebrative homecoming with new child. Whenever my wife watched it she would cry; it is an emotionally packed journey through the miracle of birth and new motherhood.

We had barely asked the question when Greta shot back in her perfect English with a deep German accent, "I *hate* that show!" Realizing that her quite forceful response could be misinterpreted, she explained: "I hate that show because

I have so many patients that watch it, and then hours after their own birth experience I'll check on them and some will start crying and say, 'I'm so disappointed, my birth was nothing like I thought it would be.' When I ask what they were expecting, they say, 'I thought it would be more like on *A Baby Story.*'"

Greta had experienced the sign being disconnected from the thing it signifies in simulation; her patients wanted their real event (giving birth) to correlate to the hyperreal, *A Baby Story's* simulation of the birth experience. They knew they were having a real experience, but they grieved that this real experience did not correlate closely enough with their simulated screen living in the hyperreal. The show is only a sign, a half-hour edited and incomplete picture of a pregnancy and birth. It is a simulation, but some people had so absorbed the sign that they had reversed things; instead of the sign pointing beyond itself to something real (like a labor that lasts eight to twelve painful hours), the sign became the thing (a romantic and sentimental half-hour trip into the miracle of birth). Having so absorbed the sign, these women had made meaning out of it: "My pregnancy and birth should be like the show," they believed. But as Greta had exclaimed, the show was not real; it was only a representation. In our screen-based world, Baudrillard asserts, the unreal screen has become the real, the hyperreal; it has made the sign, the image, into reality. This leads him to wonder if there is anything real at all. Baudrillard believes that meaning has died the death of suffocation buried under a trillion unreal and unrelated images.

THE DEATH OF MEANING

Meaning is hard to construct because when the sign and the signified are pulled apart by the hyperreal images of the screen, the line separating real from fake, subject from object, and true from false becomes blurred to such an extent that the boundary becomes indistinguishable. Which is real and which is fake—my eighteen-hour labor or the half-hour show that touches my heart? What is a person— a subject or an object to desire (to rate by appearance or to see naked)? Is my body part of my subjective person or an object to mold like the images I see? And what is true and what is false when every politician and their representative talking head on twenty-four-hour news keeps spinning and spinning an issue until I can no longer handle the dizziness? Until I no longer care what is true and what is false (for their goal isn't truth but just that I keep taking in images)? In the midst of the blur of these boundaries, meaning (i.e., what is my life and why do I live it?) becomes ever difficult to construct. The ground is always shifting as I am bombarded with new images giving me new products, perspectives, and entertainment to incorporate into my already image-saturated person.

It is not that there is no meaning; it is rather that in a world framed by screens there is *too much* free-floating meaning. There is so much possibility for meaning, but none of it seems bound to anything; it is not nailed to anything real, Baudrillard would assert. The plethora of free-floating meaning becomes too much and too confusing. Surrounded by image after image of free-floating meaning (buy this, be that, think this, want that, follow them) it all becomes noise—it all becomes meaningless. When meaning is free-floating, drifting on the winds of the hyperreal image world, it is easily popped, forcing us to scramble for some other images to consume and with which to make meaning, or else face the meaninglessness of our existence.

Life becomes consuming signs; that becomes its goal and its end. But a sign only gives direction on the road of meaning; it cannot in itself *be* meaning. We are "witness[es] to unprecedented evaporation of the grounds for meaning. The quest for some division between the real and the unreal, or even the true and untrue, moral and immoral, is futile."[3]

DISNEYLAND AND THE DEFECATING GOAT

Not long ago my family did the all-American activity of taking our children to Disneyland. We may have been too ambitious to assume that a three-year-old and a nine-month-old would be struck by the wonder of the Magic Kingdom, but we were already in Anaheim so we gave it a shot. If there is a Mecca of the hyperreal it is Disneyland. Almost nothing is real. Almost everything you can touch is a simulation of something else. Even the trees (at least the ones you can touch and climb) are cast plastic. And when the trees are real they are cut and colored toward the hyperreal.

After fighting lines with two tired kids we decided we needed a line-free low-key ride. As we walked toward Frontier Land we saw that the Tikki Room was opening for a new show. "What is this?" I asked the high-schooler in an explorer hat and kerchief in charge of ushering us in. "It's a bird show with singing," she said. I must have been delusional from the sun, but walking in I imagined real birds with real people singing. There were nets on the ceiling, which I imagined kept the birds from flying into the audience. But the room did feel small and there was no birdseed or bird feces on the floor. The room was perfectly comfortable, and there was no smell of animals. Of course the mess of stray food, bad smells, and feces would have witnessed to something real. But this was Disney; they had moved past the real, past the mess of feces. They had created a world like a dream, where the constraints of real life have no say, where animals don't sh*t and people don't suffer.

As the show started I realized why there was no mess: the birds were not real. They were mechanical simulations of birds, but better than simple simulations; these birds sang, talked, and told funny jokes. I was expecting something real, but was pushed beyond the real deeper into the Disney hyperreal.

Still needing a break after our Tikki Room experience, we followed signs toward a petting zoo. We had been in the park for hours, jumping in and out of simulated hyperreal world after hyperreal world, touching nothing real, the mess of real existence hidden behind mirrors and curtains. But as we turned the corner toward the petting zoo, the smell changed, and there it was, a real petting zoo with real (not animated or mechanical) animals. I felt my heart start to beat and my body began to twitch a little (out of fear, I guess). I had spent so much time in the Mecca of the hyperreal, climbing plastic trees, listening to singing mechanical birds, that I found myself shocked and taken aback by the fact that the goat was real. The real had punctured the hyperreal and I was overwhelmed by its presence. I kept saying to my wife, "That goat is real; the goat is real!" as she gave me the strangest of looks.

We see, in our screen worlds, more death in a month than our forefathers saw in a decade. Watching our screens we see people killed, die of cancer, be told love is over; we watch as a child falls into addiction. But the death we see has no meaning, for it is only a simulation. Even in our hospitals and funeral homes the realness of death is hidden beyond procedures in sterilized rooms that feel like simulations, concealed behind doors down corridors of rooms. The reality of death, the rustling of the monster, is ignored as we give our attention to screens, where death is only a simulation. But when death punctures our hyperreal worlds, by attacking our friend, family member, job, our own person or purpose, our thin image-based meaning system shatters. Like seeing the real goat among Disney's hyperreal, our being is shocked by the real power of the monster to destroy us, stunned to see that we have very little meaning after all.

THE CHURCH OF THE HYPERREAL

I once knew a pastor of a church who sought to be a competitor among the hyperreal, shaping his sermons like sitcoms, playing the music like pop concerts, believing that if he could compete he could offer a godly meaning system in the tones and notes of the hyperreal. Yet, often when we ask the church to play notes of the hyperreal, we hide the mess and feces of life behind fake curtains of joy, behind mirrors of moral certainty, behind the shows of religious relevance. But in a world where meaning slips away through the fissure of sign and signified, it may be that the only way to recover meaning, the only way to find something real, is to enter death, to face the monster. It may be that the only way for the church to help its people make meaning is to keep witnessing to the real amongst all the hyperreal. It is the church's proclamation amongst the buzz of the hyperreal to call out, "Don't you smell it? We are standing in sh*t! Life is messy, death is real, and we are hurting." The church must become the place where the feces of life is not quickly removed but remains present, reminding us that we are real, calling us not to make meaning out of images and simulations but out of the reality that we are dying, that we are hurting, that the monster cannot be beaten by TiVo or a new handbag.

REFLECTING ON THE STORY OF SCRIPTURE

Moses and the Exodus

The central biblical narrative of the Judeo-Christian tradition is the Exodus; the liberation from Egypt stands as the core revelatory event for the Israelites of who God is. It is in this story that they are given God's name, that they are made into a people. Abraham has been led to Canaan; he has been given a son, Isaac; but it is not until his descendants are enslaved, beaten, and crying out in utter despair that God acts to make them into a people. It is their despair that God hears. They have known God as *Elohim* (more of a generic term for God, they have known this God as the God of their fathers), but in hearing their despair God reveals

Godself anew; God reveals God's name, *Yahweh*. From their very suffering God opens God's heart, making Godself apprehendable, giving over God's name. Seeing their despair God promises to be with them in a new way, in a way that shares their suffering, in a way that will lead from their despair into a promise.

And of course the vessel God uses, the one to whom God reveals God's name, is none other than a man in despair himself—a man running, a man stuck in his shame, stuck in a foreign land, exiled, and along in years. When Moses encounters God in the burning bush and is told to return, he becomes painfully aware of the impossibility of his task. He is old, a criminal (he has killed an Egyptian), and a stutterer. But the God who hears despair sends one in despair to act for the promise for all the people.

DISCUSSION QUESTIONS

- *In what other ways do you see despair in the story of the Exodus?*

- *Tell of a time in your life or ministry where you felt in exile, lost, and beaten.*

- *This chapter has argued that meaning is hard to construct in our context due to the overabundance of images; do you have any examples of this in your life?*

- *The hyperreal often keeps us from being able to encounter the real, we can easily be overwhelmed by the real. How can your congregation invite people to live from the real? How can your church be a place that is about the real?*

CHAPTER TWO

LIFE IS LIKE A PLASTIC CUP TO BE USED AND DISPOSED OF

The Death of Authority

THIS MAY NOT COME AS A SURPRISE at this point, but I was a weird child. I did all the so-called "regular kid things" for a person of my generation. I played sports and video games and watched hours of cheesy TBS sitcoms. I also hung out with friends drinking liters of Mountain Dew, trading baseball cards, and, at dark, waterballooning cars (bored suburban kids do stupid things!). But as a kid I also spent a lot of time alone. With both parents working, I spent a lot of time thinking. When I had seen the same episode of *The Brady Bunch* or *Saved by the Bell* eleven times, I would finally turn the TV off. When I did, one of my favorite pastimes was thinking about my future. What would I do? Who would I be? Who would I marry? I still have vivid memories of lying in my bed at night thinking deeply about my future. I spent hours and hours in the summer tossing a wiffle ball to myself in my backyard, hitting it toward my house, hoping to get it on the roof for a home run. I used my made-up game to fantasize about my future, pretending I was a Major League Baseball player for the Yankees, important and famous, always dating movie stars (I guess Derek Jeter got that future).

Thinking of my future was so captivating because it was all before me. Like a huge horizon lying somewhere out before me, my future could be anything: I could mold it, I could make it into something. Aware of the constraints all around me in the present, I felt free of them when I dreamed about my future. Rejected by the pretty girl now, I would have a prettier girl in the future. A backup second baseman now, I would be an all-star in the future. The future was what I gave my attention to, for it promised me freedom and fulfillment.

And I was free—free enough to imagine my future self as I wished. I had no family trade, vocation, or business that stood ahead of me on my horizon. *You could do anything* was the seductive promise of the future. I had no entrenched connection to the land I lived on; nothing keeping me from living in Australia or anywhere else. My future love was not bound within a group of people; she wouldn't necessarily come from my little village or ethnic community but could be from anywhere. Sitting in my damp suburban basement, my ears still ringing with the silence of a room once filled with the sound of sitcom laugh tracks, I was aware that the future was wide open to me. I thought very little of the past. I had no sense that I was standing in a line of generations. I had the sense that it was just me, just me standing before a door, a door swung open that read above it, "Your Future."

I'M SICK OF THE POSTMODERN CONVERSATION—ARE YOU?

In the last ten years or so we've been bombarded with presentations and books about our cultural transitions, derivative talk after derivative chapter on modernity versus postmodernity. Even writing that last sentence made my eyelids heavy. But with all the easy (too easy) heuristic devices (e.g., "modernists are like this . . . and postmodernists are like that"), what this all comes down to in the end is a transition in how we understand ourselves in time and space. Modernity seeks to shake itself free from the rigidity of time and space. It would take nearly four hundred years to shake free, but as I could feel in my basement as a kid, it had done it. It had shaken me free. Time had shifted and space became open. This is why some social theorists don't like the word *postmodern* at all because in the end what we are dealing with is modernity at its late stage, modernity having accomplished its task of radically transforming time and space.[1]

For most of human history, space was difficult to traverse. You could only go as far as your feet or horse could take you. Most people would live and die within miles of where they were born, never leaving their kin, community, or tribe. The edge of the village or field or regular nomadic trail was the edge of the world. Modernity led to inventions like boats and trains that cross space more quickly, but it wasn't until the microprocessor, jet fuel, and satellites that space became fluid.

But modernity did more than put space in a blender; it also radically transformed time. It once took people treacherous months to years to cross the Atlantic and find their way across the plains to finally reach St. Paul, Minnesota. Often not everyone starting the voyage made it to their destination. But I can take a fifteen-minute drive, sit in a cushioned chair, watch three movies, and be in London before I can start the fourth. In a short time I have crossed huge amounts of space. " 'Far' and 'long,' just like 'near' and 'soon,' used to mean nearly the same."[2]

But it isn't the simple function of technological speed that influences us; rather, technological speed changes the way we understand ourselves in the world. Modernity, leading to late modernity, turns our attention away from the past and toward the future. For most of human history life in the present was focused on obedience to, and the continuation of, the past. You often sought to follow the way of life of your ancestors, depending on their wisdom to survive your now. We now believe past wisdom, even wisdom from the 1970s, is not only not essential, but antiquated and decrepit. Just look at Twinkies as exhibit A.

I've passed on a terrible (I can only assume genetic) deficiency to my son. He, like me, has a deep love for TV. He cycles in and out of his favorite movies (except for *Star Wars*—he never gets bored with seeing storm troopers). Last year his favorite was *Prince of Egypt*, an animated version of the Exodus story. My wife (a pastor) and I became disturbed after he watched it a few times because he kept saying, "I really like the pharaoh. I don't like Moses, I like the pharaoh." We, his theologian father and Reverend mother, felt ourselves to be in an existential parenting crisis. Every time (like forty) I watched the movie with him I was always taken aback by a line at the beginning, when Rameses, the future pharaoh is scolded by his pharaoh father: "One weak link in the chain [of generations] can bring down a dynasty!" Rameses is told that his future is about maintaining the past, recognizing that there is a chain of generations, a chain that he must honor and maintain.

It was clear, even in this kid's movie, that before modernity your destiny was first and foremost to maintain the line, to protect tradition, to keep continuity with the past. As I looked at my son, watching him watching the movie without a blink, I knew that he would have little of this concern. His dynasty was in making his *own* way in the future, unbound to the past, unbound to me. He was not a link in the chain (or only a link genetically and biologically); he was free to forget the past and make his *own* future. Our way of life encourages us to forget the past and give our attention to the future. Modernity asserts, "Old is bad and new is good. Move into the future, don't worry about the past!" Everything is new, making yesterday's wisdom old (see the diagram below).

Sitting in my basement as a kid, I gave myself over completely to the future. I knew I was not bound by space; I could live or visit anywhere. I cared little about the wisdom of my grandparents. My attention was turned completely to the future, and this, after all, was what I was supposed to be thinking about, as even teachers would remind us, pointing toward the future to motivate us for the action in the present (e.g., "Study hard now so you can go to a good college and get the job you want!"). Americans are programmed to believe that if we do all the right things, then life will work out for us—but it's not true. If we are honest with ourselves we know that even if we do all the right things, tragedy, lay-offs, separations, and depression can still happen to us.

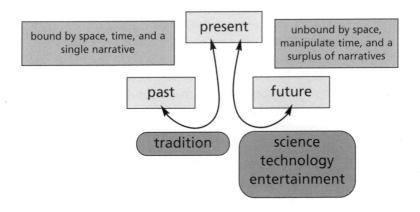

THE LOSS OF TRADITION, THE LOSS OF AUTHORITY

Modernity steps up to tradition (a way of living where authority is bound in past ways of being and doing) and punches tradition in the stomach. "All those traditional ways of being and doing don't matter, for we are about the future," modernity asserts. "We are about new inventions, new discoveries. We are about possibility. Don't seek corre-lation to the past; go and make a future for yourself." Modernity undercuts tradition. By turning our attention away from the past and toward the future, modernity makes tradition and its way of living antique—a relic of the past but not all that functional in the future.[3]

This is *not* all bad; this is in some ways, dare we say, good! Living under the burden of the past can be difficult; the free-dom of the openness of future can be liberating. I don't want anyone to take away the Internet or my satellite dish, and I like the fact that the future has many roads that I (supposedly) get to choose. Yet when modernity turns our attention away from tradition, it undercuts authority. Tradition not only organizes people's lives but also gives them answers to the questions of the universe and justification for their actions. Tradition clearly answers the question why.

Modernity gives its own answers, but they are quite different. Modernity has no patience for answers like, "If it was good enough for my father it is good enough for me," "Because we have always done it this way," "Because God says so," "Because it is in our sacred texts." Modernity believes it has outgrown these answers. Modernity asserts that questions of why will be answered in the future. But just as modernity had to bully tradition to pry open the door to the future, seeking the new and disregarding the old to complete its project of future progress, ironically modernity had to form its own zones of authority now that the past had no say on us.

But these zones of authority could not operate like past-looking traditions. Modernity, having pushed tradition to the ground by turning our chins to the future, provided us some authoritative platforms to stand on; but these needed to be platforms that operated without a past. These had to be platforms that at least seemed to be bound only by the possibilities of the future. So in the place of the authority of tradition, modernity gave us science, technology, markets, and national institutions, all which held their authority in the belief that they were clearing paths for a greater and greater future for us all.

The future was yours; you could do and be anything you wanted. Traditional, past-conforming ways of life were unneeded. Old wisdom was ignorant. Modernity's future orientation freed us from tradition, but by doing so it freed us from each other. Of course, premodern, tradition-based peoples cared about the future, but the future was a communal reality. The individual's job was not to walk into his or her future alone, but to be obedient to the ancestors and their traditions, knowing that in so doing *their* future would be bright. But in the future orientation of modernity, we are individuals free to go into the future, confident that science, technology, institutions, and markets are not only opening up the future but also helping create the future.

When two groups' desires for a future collide, it will be the one with the greater technology, markets, and national loyalty that will win and be seen as right. When two individuals find themselves in conflict, these future-orientated authorities will determine right from wrong. You can have your religion, but in conflict with science, future-orientated modernity will always side with science. Where wars were once fought to maintain a people's traditional way of life, since they feared that if their land was taken their gods would be taken too, in modernity wars are fought to assure not the continuity of the past but possibility in the future (if Vietnam falls so does capitalism, if Iraq harbored terrorists how can we be assured of a safe terror-free future?). When authority is no longer tradition but modernity's future-oriented inventions, then the individual is essential; the individual is central and authority can only be authority if it supports individuals and individual pursuits.

HERE COMES THE "POSTMODERN"

But this is where the overused and overhyped concept of "postmodernity" comes in. Once modernity enthrones science, technology, markets, and institutions as authorities without a past, allowing individuals to be central, what happens when we realize that their badges of authority are tarnished? What happens if these authorities seek their own self-preservation more than serve the future of individuals? What happens when we realize that their authority does not solve all of our problems, and worse, it makes new ones? What happens when we realize that they not only cannot slay the monster of death, but to maintain their authority they serve it, even if it means destroying individuals?

I personally find it amazing (and frightening) that I have no idea of the names of my great-grandparents. I know I could find out by asking my still-living grandmothers, but I'd bet they would have to search old documents to remember the names of their own great-grandparents. If I were offered a million dollars to give the name of one great-grandparent I wouldn't have a clue. Just three generations past and they are gone, completely forgotten. Holding my daughter, I realize that when she has grandchildren, I'll be gone; I will have been dead for years, but by the time her grandchildren can walk, I'll have been completely forgotten. It will be as though I never was. Although these future-orientated authorities of modernity can promise potential for our individual futures, it appears they provide it, ironically, by erasing us from the future. They provide an immediate voyage forward, but having turned all our gazes toward the future it is inevitable that when the monster takes us we not only are gone from the earth, but will soon be gone from memory— will soon be as though we never were.

When we realize that the authoritative platforms that modernity creates give service to the monster of death, we stand before the open door of our future with no authority. The practice of looking back to tradition has been overcome by modernity's future orientation, but now free from tradition we realize that these new authorities of modernity are no authority at all. They seek not our good, but only their own. Authority has died. Like an ambitious prince modernity has killed the king of authority (tradition) with the weapon of doubt, only to realize in shock that its own weapon has been turned against itself, destroying the new authority it constructed.

I HAVE BECOME THE NEW AUTHORITY BECAUSE I CAN DOUBT

As I peer into this future the possibilities seem endless, and what is to stop me from being or doing anything I wish? Tradition has lost its authority, as have science, technology, markets, and institutions. There is only one authority: me. I'm my own authority, for I am my end, and when I end I am gone forever. Modernity's future orientation made the individual important, but now in the vacuum of its own doubted authorities, all that is left is me. I decide what is true and what is right from my experience, feelings, and desires. On my lips I carry the most powerful of spells. I carry the question that destroys all authority in late modernity, the simple but profound, "Who says?" Who says I can't live this way? Who says that perspective isn't right? Who says this isn't true? Walking in the future, unbound by past tradition, modernity's future authorities still operating but tattered, "Who says?" becomes the magical incantation that reveals the hollowness of the future with its haunting horizon of possibility and risk that reveals that there is no path forward, only a rough terrain. The future is open. The future is yours, but it is vastly open, a dangerous horizon, for no authority is going before us. We are free, but vulnerable at every turn. Go forward, but go unprotected by any authority.

We realize, standing on the horizon of the future with authority dead, that our lives are more about fragmentation than unity. More than effortlessly surfing them, we feel like we are being forcefully pushed on the currents of the future, spitting up water as we struggle to grab for anything to stabilize us. Without an external authority, separation and division seem ever close. We can even feel it within ourselves. We have conflicting values, ways of living that we don't believe in. We act differently in different locations; sometimes we feel like two (three, four) different people.

Separation and division, the calling cards of the monster of death, can feel dangerously near in a world where authority has died. With authority dead we use knowledge as a cardboard shield to protect us from the terror of walking into an unknown future without the armor of authority. As I walk the dangerous terrain of the future without any authority, the more knowledge, information, and examples I have the better off I am. This is why the Internet is the greatest tool for those living with the death of authority (this is why we need it always available in our pockets). Without authority we have no path leading us into the future. With no path we need to acquire as much information as we can, for we never know what is right or what is wrong, what is wise and what is stupid. The more information we gather the better off we might be in the wilderness of the future. Those who can acquire the most information will be the most successful (whether that be at building their stock portfolio with stock information or keeping current with fashion trends to attract intimacy). When authority dies, knowledge multiples, for there is no longer anyone or anything to rule on its worth. When authority is undercut, we are bombarded by the escalation of information and examples on how to survive and thrive in the future. Our minds spin with their number: do this, get that, think about this. It becomes my job (every individual's job) to sift through mountains of knowledge, picking out the pieces he or she will keep. As Anthony Giddens states, "No knowledge under conditions of modernity is knowledge in the 'old' sense, where 'to know' is to be certain."[4]

When authority dies we find ourselves in the despair of too much information, too much knowledge to obtain, and too many celebrity examples to imitate. Without authority we need this information and these examples, but the hyperescalation of information and examples soon becomes more disorientating than clarifying.

YOU'RE AN ADDICT, I'M AN ADDICT

Traditions can only be traditions in collective groups. There is no such thing as individual tradition. An individual tradition is not a tradition but a habit, and when a habit is exposed to the anxiety of moving forward in a future without any authority, in the swirl of information and examples, then the habit can easily become compulsive, providing a tradition-less and authority-less individual with order. When a habit becomes compulsive, it becomes an addiction.

Addiction, Giddens believes, is itself an invention of late modernity.[5] We have seen an amazing proliferation of addictions. People can be addicted to drugs, dieting, M&Ms, watching TV, exercise, and even love. In a world without tradition many of us fall into the pit of habitual obsession, needing something to organize our frighteningly open lives. In fact, many of us (all of us) need some kind of addiction. Whereas tradition once organized our lives, we now find ourselves free—too free. The death of authority has cut us loose from any ordering principle to directly manage ourselves. We delve deeply into our schedules, careers, exercise patterns, feelings of love, or chosen drugs to organize our lives. We need some kind of addiction to give us the courage to move out into the future now that we can no longer trust science, technology, markets, and institutions. With past-looking tradition buried and the invited traditions of modernity maimed by the disease of radical doubt, we must seek some organizing habits as we apprehensively face a future were the monster of death is no longer caged behind folk rituals or institutional operations.

THE RISE OF FUNDAMENTALISM

In such a world it is no surprise that fundamentalism would appear. Maybe even in reading the above you thought, "We need to get past-looking tradition back. We need to turn back the clock." This is exactly what fundamentalism is about. It too is an invention of, or an invention made necessary by, late modernity. Fundamentalism is a response to beaten-down tradition.

Fundamentalism is a desire to return to an authority now that authority is dead. It is a chest-beating, vigorous assertion that there is an authoritative foundation in a world where authority has been killed. Fundamentalism provides people an authoritative place to stand beyond doubt. It is no wonder that fundamentalism is on the rise; it offers people smelling the stench of dead authority (a death that brings their own impending death to the surface) a way of living that need not always wrestle with radical doubt. It provides people bombarded by storms of doubt (which we all are) and the loss of meaning a safe harbor. Fundamentalism offers protection from the monster; all you have to do to get it is give the fundamentalist perspective or person your total devotion without doubt or question. But you can only do this if you deny the monster, if you act as though not even death has victory over the fundamentalist perceptive or person.

And this is the major problem with fundamentalism. To maintain its integrity, and therefore protect people from the death of authority, it must maintain its singular authoritative vision even if it means killing (physically, spiritually, emotionally, or intellectually) those who do not hold its perspective. In a pluralistic world, fundamentalism claims singularity. In a complicated world where death and a plethora of questions, doubts, and fears confront us all, fundamentalism has no room for such things, for it possesses truth and it damns anyone who sees it otherwise. Then, just as ironically, as modernity invented zones of authority so it could kill the authority of tradition, fundamentalism must kill (again, physically, spiritually, emotionally, and intellectually) to maintain the integrity of its airtight authority. In order to have its authority, fundamentalism must serve the monster it intended to overcome. It must serve the monster while giving it ultimate power; it feeds it while ignoring its bloodthirsty presence.

THE CHURCH, FUNDAMENTALISM, AND OTHER RESPONSES

Although there are a handful of churches and ministries that have dealt with the death of authority by taking on fundamentalism, there has been another strategy as well. That strategy, whether operated by mainline liberal congregations or newer emergent type communities, has been to walk around the death of authority by embracing cultural pluralism. Many of the mainline liberal congregations that I know have often taken on the ideological perspective of openness (yes, I do mean that as an oxymoron), just as many of the emergent communities I am aware of have sought to make church relevant to the style of the constantly future-directed cultural surfers. Both, from my perspective, are better options than fundamentalism. Yet what all three do is make knowledge and examples essential. This, after all, is the way to survive our future-orientated lives where authority has dissolved. Knowledge and examples are central whether that be the unquestionable knowledge of the Bible and TV healers, a liberal ideological perspective on openness, or knowledge about cultural transitions and new forms of doing church and the example of their representative congregations and pastors.

Unlike fundamentalists, most mainline liberals and emergent communities recognize that old dogmatism—whether about sexuality, doctrine, or worship style—is doubted and doubted deeply, but in the end they often offer us more knowledge, information, and examples.

I know of a church in a university town whose youth group takes great pride in their openness but despises narrow people who are "too into Jesus." Mainline liberals are just as ideological as before, only now instead of being ideological about their possession of a particular truth (e.g., their assertion that the twentieth century would be the Christian century) they are ideological about how much

35

more open and intellectual they are than conservatives. To revitalize themselves they just need to get that information out. Although some emergent communities recognize that there is no *de facto* authority in institutions and denominations anymore, they nevertheless have provided us with more knowledge, information, and examples of a new style of church through blogs, websites, and conferences (and, of course, books like this one).

Yet, what none of them—fundamentalism, mainline liberalism, or emergent communities—seem to do is make their life *in* the death of authority, to seek faith only in doubt, to find God not by circumventing the death of authority with more knowledge, but somewhere in its death. What the church needs in a world where authority has died are people brave enough to enter the sea of doubt and seek not for a lost authority, new ideology, or a more relevant style, but for a God found in despair.

So what if, instead of looking for some place to stand amongst the death of authority, some sliver of knowledge to hold to in the storm, some example to follow, we simply let go? What if instead of trying to acquire knowledge we focused on being people who were brave enough to see death in its fullness? What if instead of seeking to make some sense out of the death of authority, we made our home there? What if we became the people who said yes. Yes, it is true. There is no authority and the future is dangerously unpredictable and we are not sheltered from the monster by anything; we are exposed. Our inerrant Bible, ideology, or relevance will not help; let's face it, death is on the way and we will soon be gone and forgotten forever. Let us let go and admit it. But let's let go and trust as well, trust that in facing death (the death of meaning and death of authority) we will encounter a paradox that cannot be bound by knowledge or stellar examples. In the mystery of being, in the mystery of letting go and giving ourselves over to despair, we will not acquire more or better knowledge, but instead we'll come up against the very being of a crucified God.

REFLECTING ON THE STORY OF SCRIPTURE

David

All the nations surrounding the Israelites have kings. Their economies and militaries seem so much stronger than the small nation of Israel. They are so technologically advanced. Their kings give them an authority, a way to galvanize the people, something the tribal people of Israel do not have. Now they want a king of their own. They want an authority, someone to lead them. The prophet Samuel continues to remind them that power always corrupts and it won't be long until this authority of theirs squeezes them where it hurts, sending their children to war and taking their crops as taxes. But they feel lost, and they demand authority.

The handsome and tall Saul is chosen—Saul who looks like a king, who embodies authority. But the God of the Exodus has not shown God's favor for Saul. The God who moves from despair, the God who reveals God's name to those in pain, the God who picks stutterers to be God's mouthpiece finds no favor with the tall and muscular, gives no preference to the authoritative. And of course, soon Israel needs a new king, but this time God will anoint a king according to the way God has revealed Godself in the Exodus, the God of the people of despair. So Samuel goes to a family with sons strong, tall, and powerful, but none of them is the one. It is revealed that little David, the one too insignificant to be fetched for the arrival of the prophet, the one who daydreams and sings, the little one who his father never dreamed would be anything but a shepherd boy, is the God of the Exodus's choice. The boy who sings songs of lament and songs of joy is to be king, the boy whose name is all over a book with songs and poems like Psalm 88:

O LORD, God of my salvation,
   when, at night, I cry out in your presence,
let my prayer come before you;
   incline your ear to my cry.
For my soul is full of troubles.
. . .
But I, O LORD, cry out to you;
   in the morning my prayer comes before you.
O LORD, why do you cast me off?
   Why do you hide your face from me?
Wretched and close to death from my youth up,
 I suffer your terrors; I am desperate.
Your wrath has swept over me;
   your dread assaults destroy me.
They surround me like a flood all day long;
   from all sides they close in on me.
You have caused friend and neighbor to shun me;
   my companions are in darkness. (vv. 1-3, 13-18)

The boy who was too small for Israelite armor, who miraculously killed the giant with an insignificant rock, will rule the people from a heart that sings of pain and despair but always trusts in God's promises.

DISCUSSION QUESTIONS

- *What rationality do you see in God choosing the insignificant to rule? How does this change the way we think about power?*

- *Do you have a most significant psalm? What is it and why is it significant to you?*

- *In this chapter I argued that when tradition doesn't organize our lives knowledge becomes central, but knowledge is always contested. Where do you see this in our world? What information do you trust? Why do you trust this information?*

- *How then does the church become a trustworthy place to people in our world (e.g., through better information, recovering a traditional way of life, or as I argue, sharing in our suffering in despair)?*

CHAPTER THREE

THE ATTACK OF THE ZOMBIES

The Death of Belonging

I MUST HAVE BEEN FOUR OR FIVE years old. It probably was within months of Benjamin's death. I couldn't have been much older, because we would move to a new house by the end of kindergarten. I was only four or five, but I remember vividly having free rein. I remember being blocks away from home with no adults present, hanging out with other children. I remember walking to the nearby junkyard and hauling back old rusted metal and nail-filled boards to build an airplane (it never flew, but we really believed in our five-year-old imaginations that it might). I remember darting out of the house to roam freely, exploring all sorts of dangerous things in our newly built suburban neighborhood that was still surrounded by farmland and old silos. I was five and had free rein. And it wasn't that my parents were negligent; there were kids everywhere, filling this neighborhood of starter houses. And we all were free to ride our bikes streets away. We were free to go as far as yelling distance.

My son is quickly approaching five, and I simply can't imagine allowing him to do the same. I can't imagine my five-year-old being blocks from our house, with no adult nearby to watch him. In conversation with my friend one day my unease was confirmed. He explained how busy life is with two children ten and eight. "Most of my life is driving them from one play date to another; from lessons to practices, our calendar is packed." And then he continued,

"It's not like when we were kids, when we could roam, when we were told, 'Just don't cross that busy road or go through the park, and be home by 5:00.' "

His lament got me thinking, why? Why in the last few decades have we shifted from kids (even small ones) free to roam our neighborhoods to kids (even older ones like ten-, eleven-, and twelve-year-olds) needing to be under constrained supervision, even within the parameters of organized play dates?

I suppose at least in part that the media has convinced us that in the last three decades the world has become a much more dangerous place. But the truth is that in most neighborhoods and communities crime is down, not up. It could be argued that our neighborhoods are safer than they were three decades ago. Our neighborhood is as safe as the neighborhood I grew up in (it may be safer: there are no junkyards to trudge through or abandoned silos that I could fall down). So why are we so much more afraid? Even knowing the facts, why would I refuse to let my son roam my neighborhood?

I think it has everything to do with the fact that we don't know our neighbors anymore. The last three decades have not become more dangerous, but they have become riskier, not because the world is suddenly flooded with pedophiles, burglars, and child abductors, but because we have lost more and more civic or communal connection to each other. My parents could be pretty confident that, even streets away, when someone saw me they knew where and to whom I belonged. If I was doing something stupid or criminal (like when I knocked down a bird's nest and smashed the eggs—I still feel bad about that), one of the adults around would call me by name and say that they would tell my parents. They knew my parents—at least they knew where they lived. Truth be told, I not only don't know most of the people in my neighborhood, I only know a few folks on my own street. If my son were blocks away, most people would have no idea who he was and where he belonged. Not recognizing him, they would have little incentive or even awareness to make sure he was OK and didn't do something stupid (which I am aware is a genetic trait). The world is not more dangerous, but it has become riskier because communal belonging has died.[1]

RISK

In a hyperreal world where tradition has been lost, we are thrust into risk. The world isn't more dangerous than it was decades or centuries earlier, but it is riskier. Risk is different from danger. Danger is having your village raided by bandits; risk is knowing that on the freeway another car could come over the median at any moment. But every day you risk it; you have subconsciously calculated the risk and the odds are with you. In a world of constant risk it is no wonder that risk-based leisure sports like base-jumping have escalated, both in creation and participation.[2]

Risk is the ever-present possibility that, with a few wrong moves and some bad luck, your life as you know it could fall apart. Risk is understanding that your life is up to you, that you are held by little else besides your decisions and your ability to avoid the ever-present threats of life. Life has always been dangerous, but in most places in most times, unlike our own, you were held in the net of a community, kin group, or village. If tragedy struck, the community knew how to deal with it. Your destiny was dependent not on your singular choice, for in many places in the past the sole individual had few choices. Risk is, in effect, living beyond the all-encompassing belonging of community.

Now free from the all-encompassing community, we are overwhelmed with individual choice (what to buy, whom to date, where to work, how to invest, what to eat—things once decided by the tradition-based community). Given all of this, individual choice means dealing with risk as a way of life. You can eat what you want, but you risk heart disease. You can spend the money you have (or don't have, with credit), but you risk deep debt and no retirement. You can love whom you wish, but you risk painful breakup. And even when wanting to avoid these risks, we're struck with the fact that even the experts disagree on how. Some say a glass of red wine is good for you; others say never drink any alcohol. Danger has meaning attached to it; we suffer because we have denied our ancestors. Danger lives with authority; though this is dangerous we must obey. But risk exists in a vacuum of meaning (it is your sole choice) and authority (even the experts disagree). Danger faces the monster, but risk plays the odds and gambles that we can avoid the monster.

In a hyperreal world without tradition we become human calculators of risk. We are asked individually to calculate the risk level of each of the decisions we make and the relationships we have. It's like the commercials for home security systems (that I must admit work on me), where the young, perfect suburban couple is just enjoying a night of relaxation after putting their kids to bed when a man dressed in black kicks in their door or breaks a window. The alarm sounds, the burglar runs away, and the phone rings. It is the soothing voice of a security company operator, "Help is on its way." The beautiful family is safe.

Let's face it, the chances of some bad guy kicking in your door while you're home in the middle-American neighborhood depicted in the commercial are almost nil. But (and here is where the alarm companies get people) why risk it? You can lower your risk index significantly if you simply pay thirty-five dollars a month—isn't that worth it? And there are multiple other ways to lower your risk index, like driving a SUV so when that car comes over the median he eats your grill, not you his. Assessing risk is a growing business, whether for individuals or corporations.

TRUST

But no matter how much risk assessment I get, Ulrich Beck and Anthony Giddens remind me that I still have to trust. We have heard the little lie that we don't need the blind trust of the past so often that we mostly believe it. It is the lie that in a modern world life is supported by the beams of dependability. We know why weather changes—no need to trust in the deity. We have science— you don't need to trust in old rituals for safety in your pregnancy. But the truth is that in the modern (late-modern) world blind trust is needed more than in the tradition-based community. The tradition-based community may have asked for our uncritical trust in their practices and beliefs, but today we do something even riskier: we trust in the operations of corporations, markets, bureaucracies, and institutions that, unlike tradition, have not been tested by time or held together by a shared narrative of a shared community. I must simply trust in the midst of risk. When I get my tires changed I must trust that the mechanic whom I have never met and who cares little whether I live or die will tighten my bolts. When I have my paycheck electronically deposited into my bank account and then see the number on a computer screen, I have to trust that all the money is really there. I must trust that when I grab a pack of ground beef in the supermarket it will not make my children sick. I have no idea where it has come from, who touched it, and how it was prepared. I read the label "pure lean ground beef" and trust. It is risky, but even if I go all organic I still have to face the risk of trust.

Ultimately, risk is about avoiding the pitfalls and traps of the monster of death. We are tempted to believe that if we simply have enough knowledge, money, and opportunity we can make a path for ourselves that circumvents the monster's snares; that if we have enough money in the bank it won't matter if we are laid off; that if our kids are in good schools we avoid the risk of their demise. Even some forms of religion are never about facing the monster of death, as most now dead communities once did through festivals or religious practice, but about finding the individual trail where risk is at its least and therefore the monster is less threatening. Too often Christianity has become risk insurance; it is *not* about facing the monster but about something good to do just in case (youth pastors know how often parents think of youth group like this). Something that seems to keep the monster away, something that gives you good luck as you face a life of risk. Life is a gamble, and in a world of individual risk management, where all-encompassing community has gone the way of the dodo bird, church and faith can easily become a placebo to mitigate the anxiety of risk. The world is *not* becoming more secular, but nevertheless religion has radically changed for Western people. It has changed from being about a community facing life and death to being a charm to carry as we toss the dice of life—hoping our church attendance and religious practice keeps us from snake eyes and the appearance of the bloodthirsty monster.

This risk is not just personal and individual but reaches deeply into how our whole society is structured. We enjoy the benefits of nuclear power but know that using this power comes with the risk of pollution or the catastrophic failure of a nuclear winter. Machines that quickly net tons of fish provide jobs and industry but come with the risk that one day the ocean will run out of fish. As a global society we have moved from natural danger to manufactured risk. We worry about global warming and the melting of the Arctic shelf—not natural dangers but manufactured risk created by us. Hurricanes are increasing because of the warming of sea waters, and we risk catastrophe for building cities on earthquake fault lines. For millions of years people feared the danger of the natural world; we now fear the risks of what we have done to the world. This is an altogether new kind of despair (a kind of despair having its birth after the Manhattan Project) that realizes that the natural world itself is at risk of death.

FROM COMMUNITIES TO INSTITUTIONS

When the all-encompassing circle of community and tradition is broken by modernity's future orientation, we find ourselves free from the constraints of day-to-day communal life. We find ourselves free to be and act as we please, no longer needing to correlate ourselves to the rules, practices, and perspective of a collective group.

When this happens, we turn over the job of ordering our social world from communities to institutions. Institutions are much better prepared to organize future-orientated life because they don't operate from a past-looking tradition. They exist not to bring people together, but to provide the freedom to live our individual lives in the future. It is institutions, and not communities, that we depend upon. It is institutions that don't know my name (most know me as number) or my story (only my balance or record) that I have built my life around. It seems that I can live without my parents or friends but not without my ATM card, drivers license, and Internet access. I can live without knowing anything about my great grandparents but I must know my Social Security number and credit rating.

When our lives become about risk management rather than facing danger in communities, we give over the fundamental operations of our lives to institutions. Who would take care of my family if I died in the next few years? Who would make sure my mortgage was paid and my wife had money to maintain her life? Not my community, not my church, not even my extended family. They may all help, dropping off a casserole and offering a shoulder to cry on, but their job, we assume, would be emotional support. No, if I died it would not be a community that would take care of my kids and wife; it would be an institution, the insurance company I've been paying to provide for them if the monster takes me sooner rather than later. For most of human history this was the work of the community: widows and orphans were to be cared for by uncles, aunts, and neighbors. Their emotional, but most fundamentally their basic financial and material, needs were the responsibility of those who knew them and were part of their story. This was not easy and I'm sure a burden, but it was dependable and communal.

What we often know but rarely articulate is that trusting an institution, even if we have been paying it to care for our families if we die early or can't work because of an accident, is in itself risky. More and more often these risk-protecting institutions called insurance companies have been failing us, finding ways not to pay. And there is little we can do if they find a loophole. And so my battle with cancer would leave my wife not only without a husband but also hundreds of thousands of dollars in debt.

ZOMBIE INSTITUTIONS

What do we do, and what is our future, when institutions continue to show us they cannot be trusted to care for anything other than their own survival? Just think of the large institutions that have failed us in this decade: corporations (such as Enron, Lehman Brothers, AIG), the church (for example, the Catholic Church abuse scandal), financial markets (the housing crisis), newspapers (for example, Jayson Blair of the *New York Times* making up stories about Iraq), intelligence (9/11), governmental response (Katrina), and the presidential office (weapons of mass destruction in Iraq). Most of our institutions are what Ulrich Beck calls "Zombie institutions."[3] They are still moving and breathing, but they have become more haunting than helpful because they are more dead than alive. Standing in late modernity there is more than a little despair knowing that we cannot go back to the tradition-based community, but that the institutions of modernity are ghouls.

As in all good horror movies, what zombie institutions do is infect all of our places of belonging, striking them with the scent of death. Institutions no doubt bring people together (many of us met our spouses in college or grad school), but the institution's primary objective is not to form deep communal connection but to bestow a degree, make money, or keep order (depending on what kind of institution it is). Once it has fulfilled its task or is kept from doing so, the connections we have built through the institution are over, and if they are to continue they must take on a new form.

At my school there was a group of six young women who met the first week of their first year. They became deep friends, creating a rich community of belonging. They ate together every Sunday night, shared in each other's pain and tragedy, and celebrated with every joy. They created a deep community that changed each of them. And this community had its genesis in the fact that an institution, our school, had brought them together. They would never have known each other, or shared life together so deeply, if not for Luther Seminary. Luther's apartment building became their sanctuary of meeting, their place of prayer and conversation. Without the institution there would have been no deep community of belonging (and their community was deep).

But something happened as the first semester of their final year was coming to an end; you could see it on each young woman's face. Their community was given a terminal countdown. They had deep community, but beyond the will of each of them, it was going to end; one more semester and it was over. For the next four months they mourned. They had grown together so much, loved each other so deeply, but with graduation it would be over. Sure, they would remain friends, still to this day meeting in Las Vegas or other places to reconnect, but now more as a reunion than a community, now more to catch up than to bear existence with each other. The institution had brought them together, giving them the space to form deep community, but that was not the institution's primary objective. So just as the institution giveth community, it taketh it away.

THE EXPIRATION DATE OF COMMUNITY

And this is true for almost all of us. Almost every community we form in the hyperreal world of late modernity comes with an expiration date. You can have deep belonging (I'm not denying this), but this belonging comes with an either explicit or implicit ending. We can have deep belonging, but once one of you has a child, everything changes; once you get a promotion you will move; once you have finished your basement you will no longer need your help group. There are many places and many options to form community, but almost all of them come with the warning label, "This belonging is belonging until further notice." There are many options for belonging—but they all are very risky, for they all promise that they will end, and sometimes painfully. There is a temporality to the place of belonging in our world, a temporality to belonging that makes it at times not feel much like belonging at all. There is death in the marrow of our communities.

Institutions bring us together, allowing us to form belonging with one another, but they cannot (in order to keep their future orientation) serve this connection—they must serve the objective for their creation (and often badly). Institutions exist for functions (to give you your license, provide a service, etc.), not for what sociologists call "expressive relationships" (relationships for relationship's sake). This puts us in quite a bind. In late modernity the all-encompassing traditional community is dead; it has been punctured by modernity's future orientation and its carcass eaten by swarms of images in the hyperreal. We therefore find the belonging we need to be human through institutions; we meet our friends and lovers at work, school, or the bar. And when meeting these people we form deep relationship, significant belonging. But the objective of most institutions is to pull us apart again. We have a plethora of options for belonging, but unlike the tradition-based community, which was solid as a rock (both for good and bad), belonging for us is liquid. It can individually quench a great thirst, but sooner or later will leave us parched again.

COMMUNITIES' SECRET SAUCE: OBLIGATION

Why is this? Why is rock solid community impossible for us? Because it is based on obligation, and obligation is a dirty word for those of us living in late modernity (I personally hate it). Community cannot be community where individual free will is king. Community demands that I give up my own freedom for the good of the group. Therefore, lasting community asks that I see myself obligated to these people (my belonging is deeper than my job, education, place of residence, or personal identity—I choose the community over it). But we don't see things this way; rather, we expect our communities not to come before these personal things, but to serve us (personally) by enhancing them. Gerard Delanty states that "we need to ask whether 'community beyond tradition,' . . . or what William Corlett (1993) calls 'community without unity,' can be possible."[4]

When it is solely my free will to choose a community there is the great benefit that I feel that it is mine, that it is part of me. But in the end there is nothing keeping me there but my sole choice. If at any time my preference, style, or taste changes, I'm gone. It is hard to have rich community amidst such fluidity. Without obligation, community will always be short-lived. Community throughout history has been based on the necessity of obligation. In late modernity, in our time, we are trying something never done before: we are trying to have belonging in community based not on obligation but on feelings. I'm in community when I feel it! These feelings give me great desire and wonderful experiences; the problem is, of course, that feelings often fade.

Community cannot be lasting when it is based on preference, style, and taste. I can't choose community like I choose my favorite coffee shop (though we often try). I choose my favorite coffee shop because I like the atmosphere, the people seem interesting, and the coffee is good (or good enough). I don't feel obligated. If the decor changes or I switch from coffee to smoothies, I'm under no obligation to remain loyal. Maybe feeling a little sentimental, I simply move on. Our communities may feel like places where we really belong, but they are very easy to move on from, because they are based in our preference and taste, not in obligation. This is good, but risky. I like that I can easily choose in or out. But what happens if the monster gets me? What happens if I become so maimed that I become a burden to the community? What happens if those ravaged by seeing the monster face-to-face, those suffering from schizoid episodes, fill our communities? Will we stay? Will the community still exist? Or in other words, can a group of people face death even in the pits of hell and remain together? What will keep them together? Preference, taste, and style are no match for the monster.

THE CHURCH AND COMMUNITY

Community has become a buzzword within the church; it is one of the essential marks of the emergent church sensibility. We have realized that in our world we must be more about community than denominational bureaucracy, more about places of belonging than places of airtight doctrine. This is all good and right, except that we have rarely explained what we mean by community and what it is that will keep us together.[5] Is it the music? The preaching? The location? The children's ministry? The people? I presume we would say the people, but what about the people? That they're cool? Interesting? What in the end holds the church together? In a world without obligation it would be hard to force community to be formed around obligatory structure (through some are doing this, whether asserting the need for doctrinal purity or through particular practice like the catechumenate or New Monasticism). But for most of us, in the end community is just about the feeling of belonging. But, again, feelings fade.

I wonder if there are not many who would love to be in community, who enter our buildings or meeting areas and feel nothing, who have been so beaten up by life and experiences of death that they feel nothing. I wonder if there are not many who see us in our moments of community worship and community fellowship and wonder if we have really dared to see and admit how alone we really are and how deeply painful loneliness is. Psychologists say that patients have the hardest time talking about loneliness because loneliness is the closest feeling to the annihilation of death.

We have something called community, feelings of liking to be together. Church is about community, we say. But does the church and its packaging of community simply hide us from what is true deep inside of us? Does our thin feeling of community sedate us from the reality of our loneliness? We have shouted to the world that church is about community; the church of the future will not be about institutions or doctrine but about being together. We have shouted this, but maybe this is not what we should be shouting. Maybe we should be shouting, with so many others in world, that we are lonely, that we are alone, that death kills all in our communities and we are scared. Maybe the world does not believe because we have offered personal options for community instead of belonging in a community that knows and speaks of the despair of loneliness. Maybe the only way to form a community that can withstand preference, style, and taste is not to base it on feelings of togetherness but on naming and bearing the despair of our shared loneliness.

REFLECTING ON THE STORY OF SCRIPTURE

Sarah

A promise has been given to her husband. He has been promised that he will be the father of a great nation, as great in numbers as the sand on the shore. From his promise one has been given to her: if he is the father of a nation then she will be the mother; she (especially in her context) will then be the richest of people, the most blessed of all women. The promise has been given, but remains unmet. The promise has been given, but now it serves as a weight that only gives exclamation to her despair. She is without child, she has nothing, he is cursed. She is meaningless, for she is barren and to be barren is to be worth nothing; it is to be in despair. And yet the promise still comes, but comes as further curse, for though it speaks of her having children, she is now *way* past the years of childbearing. But out of her despair, out of her barren womb, God will bring the fulfillment of God's promise. From Sarah it is revealed that this God, this God who calls Abram from his father's house, this is a God who waits until there is no possibility (a dead womb in a ninety-year-old woman) to act. The promise is connected to the despair; it is from the despair of Sarah's dead womb that life comes. The young fertile womb of Hagar is no good for this God of despair. This God chooses the impossible to bring forth the possible; this God chooses to bring life from death.

DISCUSSION QUESTIONS

- *Why do you think God waits until Sarah is way past the childbearing age to open her womb?*

- *Have there been times in your life where from barrenness God has acted? Explain.*

- *This chapter argued that a number of institutions are failing and that we have turned most of our lives over to institutions. How have you see this in your context?*

- *In your location, how do you imagine, or in what actions would, a church seek to be a community by helping people articulate their loneliness?*

CHAPTER FOUR

HELLO! I'M MY BODY

The Death of Identity

M Y WIFE AND I LIVED in Melbourne, Australia, for three months. We moved into a flat on the campus of the Whitley Baptist College and immersed ourselves in the local culture. We rode the tram, walked the park, and made a weekly visit to Queen Victoria Market (every week I was as fascinated as the previous week with the ground kangaroo meat). We found ourselves in long conversations with locals and watched a ton of Australian television (I became hooked on the soap opera *Neighbours*, but it doesn't take much to get me hooked on TV shows). But the truth be told, the three months were a mix of exhilarating experiences and mind-numbing boredom. It was exhilarating to explore a new place, to talk with different people, and to see new sights. But after the fun was over and the weekly budget was spent we found ourselves with long hours and nothing to do. With only an all-day cricket test match on TV (and believe me, I tried hard to watch and understand), the boredom would sweep us up into nostalgia for home. After staring for hours at the wall, we would walk the streets bored and a little depressed. In those moments homesickness would set in with severe force.

I suppose there was some benefit to this heavy boredom. We were forced to think about our lives, and like good citizens of late modernity we contemplated our futures. With everything we owned back home in a six-by-ten storage site, no jobs, and in our mid-twenties, it was clear we needed to figure out who we were and what was next.

It was in Melbourne, in that homey but dirty little flat (the carpet gave us athlete's foot), that we decided what we would do with our lives. We formulated identities for ourselves. After our three months in Melbourne we traveled for three more months in the Middle East and Europe. We would meet people and when they would ask what we did we would shoot into our new-formed identities. My wife would be a pastor and I would be an academic theologian. At first it seemed so odd. Of course we had gifts, and I guess you could say a calling in these directions, but ultimately these new identities as would-be pastor and professor we chose by ourselves. No one forced us to see ourselves in these ways; we freely chose these new identities. Sitting in a little dirty apartment, feeling oppressed by every minute of a Sunday afternoon, we picked our identities. In the swirl of the mundane, as kids outside on an altogether forgettable Sunday afternoon played cricket against their garage door like I once played baseball, *we chose* who we would be.

But thinking about who we would be when we returned, creating these identities for ourselves, only made us more homesick. When we simply couldn't take it anymore, when the boredom and homesickness got to be too much, we would do a very odd thing. In a little shopping center a few miles from our flat was a Kmart. And when we had too much we would go to Kmart to lick our homesick wounds. Somehow the smells and sounds of consumerism soothed our weariness. Feeling overwhelmed and depressed we would soak our wounds in the aisles of consumer goods. I guess it felt the most like home to simply take in the electricity of the consumer marketplace, to be surrounded by things, many of which no one needed. But buying them provided their consumers with something: identity. Just as we were working out our identities, feeling ourselves far away from anything solid, far away from things like home, family, and friends, the stuff in Kmart called out to us. It whispered that it could help, that it would help in the now. In the midst of feeling so out of place, as foreigners in a strange land, the liturgy of consumerism made us feel like ourselves. We could have been anywhere; inside Kmart we could have been in Mississippi, Los Angeles, or Melbourne. The sounds, smells, and practices (as well as most of the products) were all the same. Sure, we had plans for who we would be, but the stuff in the aisles could help us now—it could help us pick and communicate who we were, when it all felt up for grabs. This stuff could free us from our boredom; it could make us into something, it whispered.[1]

CREATING YOUR OWN IDENTITY
FROM WORK AND LOVE

The day modernity punctured the all-encompassing traditional community a new reality was born for individuals. It became our job to formulate an identity, to discover or more accurately, especially in late modernity, to *create* who we are. For most of human history you had little choice of who you were and minimal options to change your fortune. Now a peasant, forever a peasant. Many historians tell us there was little thinking at all about identity. Few people thought much about their subjective selves. It wouldn't be until the sixteenth and seventeenth centuries that personal journals would become common. Searching your inner thoughts and feelings to know who you were was absurd. Your tradition, whether religious or cultural, told you who you were by telling you who you would marry and what you would do. You knew your place and there was little need to think beyond it.

Identity is an invention of modernity. From its future orientation we are freed to be who we desire. As modernity frees us to seek the future it gives us also the freedom to be who we want, to see ourselves in a way best suited for our future. In the early part of the twentieth century it was believed that you discovered your identity as you reached out into the future and discovered your own (individual) skills and abilities (this is why it was thought that adolescence was the time of identity formation, because it was a time when your future was right before you, when you would cross the threshold of graduation and enter the rest of your life). At fifteen you discovered you were good at math, science, or breaking into cars. These skills and abilities became the building blocks for your identity; they became what you would be and do for the rest of your life. If you were good at math you went to college, majored in accounting, graduated, became an accountant, got a job doing the books for a business, got a gold watch, and retired. Your identity, the way you knew yourself, was as an accountant. If someone asked, "Who are you?" You might say, "I'm Bill. I'm an accountant." Your self-definition revolved around your work.

But it wasn't just work that formed your identity; it was also your love. Somewhere between fifteen and twenty years old you would find your sweetheart, fall in love, marry her (or him), have three kids, buy a house, and start volunteering for the PTA or coaching Little League. You knew yourself not only as accountant but also as a husband or wife, as a father or mother. In the future-oriented push of modernity you discovered your own identity through work and love (it is no wonder then that Freud would say that a healthy person is someone who can work and love). To have a solid identity is to have solid work and solid love.

THE MELTING OF WORK AND LOVE

But the solidity of work and love would melt quickly in the blur of late modernity. Identity has always been a freely chosen self-definition in search of the future. But what happens when work and love are no longer dependable? What happens when the very material to form an identity (something only done after tradition, mind you) becomes hollow?

Work and love have not held up well in late modernity,

making identity thin, making it harder and harder to have *one* self-definition. There is really no such thing any more as deciding at fifteen that you're good at something and becoming that; there is no such thing as getting a job in your major and staying with the same company for fifty years. The rapid technological changes make your education obsolete in a few years; the rapid shifting, downsizing, and morphing of corporations makes lifelong loyalty as quaint as the mimeograph machine.

The statistics are always changing but the phenomena to which they point are not: Americans change careers, on average, every twenty months. Not jobs, but careers, doing something completely different than you did in your last job, every twenty months. College students are now getting pep talks from their parents about making themselves competitive, not by being an expert at something but by being adaptable. It is no longer important to be good at one thing and loyal to one company, but to be able to quickly change.[2]

Love too has shown signs of rot. Where once it was one love for one man or woman, this is becoming more and more uncommon. Late marriage and high divorce rates make it very unlikely that anyone falls in love once and stays with that person forever. Most people love more than once in their lifetime. Just as work has become about adaptability and constant transition, so has love.

When work and love are constantly transitional, so too is identity. My self-definition changes when I change jobs or lovers; I know myself differently, see the world differently, and in many ways become a different person. Identity becomes fluid when work and love are liquefied. They still exist, no doubt, but they have greatly transformed, no longer able to support a single self-definition.

THE SHIFT: FROM WORK TO CONSUMPTION

In late modernity it is no longer work and love (as Freud had argued) that provide an identity; rather, the building blocks of identity have shifted from work to consumption. It is no longer important what you do; what is important is what you can buy. I have a friend who hates, and I mean hates, when someone asks him what he does. He feels like it's a violation of his person. "I'm more than where I work," he'll say, exasperated, but he never shies away from discussing his new electronic gadgets.

We often form identity not through vocation but through our possessions: for example, I'm the kind of person who lives in this kind of neighborhood and drives that kind of car; I'm not sure what she does, but it has gotten her that house. Consumption works within the fluid transitions of modernity to provide identity better than work does, for consumption not only holds the integrity of the future-orientation of modernity, but radicalizes it by making the future all that is important, allowing us to quickly change and morph our identities by changing our future consumer patterns. In the fluidity of late modernity all I need is a stop at Target, the Gap, or the Apple store to feel like a new person. I use what I buy to define myself. And with easy (too easy) credit I can consume without even having money. Consumption has replaced work to such an extent that I no longer even need work (or money for that matter) to consume. I just find what I want and hand over my MasterCard (priceless!). I can, at least until my creditors catch up with me, live in the unreality of consuming without the reality of work or money.

THE SHIFT: FROM LOVE TO INTIMACY

Love was once believed to be as solid as a rock, but the friction of late modernity has washed over it with such speed that it has become brittle. We still desire love. We are overwhelmed with romantic comedies and pop love songs, but ultimately our attention is not on love (a constant commitment to each other) but on intimacy, on the feelings of closeness. We base both our romance and our friendships on feelings of intimacy.

For many early-twentieth-century couples, love and feelings of intimacy were not always congruent; how you felt had little determination on the state of your love. Love was about commitment; love was about constancy and dependability. But in late modernity you can love your spouse or partner and yet feel a void of intimacy that in the end justifies you moving on and finding someone else to provide the intimacy you desire. It is not unusual to hear someone say, "I still love him, there was just nothing there" (translation: no intimacy); "I guess in the end we were just different people" (translation: my identity changed and my desired future was different from his).

The transition from identity being built on work and love to consumption and intimacy has the advantage of allowing us the freedom to quickly adapt to the future, changing our very self-definition with new information and new belonging. It is so fluid that it can even allow us to have different self-definitions in contact with different information and with different groups of belonging. Consumption and intimacy have the great benefit (unlike work and love) of not being heavily time possessive. Consumption and intimacy take little time—just a slide of the credit card or the gaze from another, the response of your fluttering heartbeat, and you are in the land of new identity; you are ready to define yourself differently.

Basing identity on consumption and intimacy instead of work and love is neither time possessive nor space directed. When consumption and intimacy are the source for identity, then we are free from concerning ourselves with any particular place. Consumption can be done from anywhere and intimacy needs only the contact of two, but nothing else.

THE DARK SIDE

While identity based on consumption and intimacy has its advantages, it also has a dark side—a dark side that smells much like the nothingness that death promises.

When identity is constructed in the constant flow of consumption and intimacy, it can often feel like there is little to hold on to. In the rush of consumption and the constant transitions in intimacy, it feels as if I could fall into a dark pit. With the diminishing pleasure of every new thing I buy and the atrophy of every new intimate relationship, I feel the monster at my back, whispering a hideous assertion in my ear: "You don't know who you are, do you? Now that death's wear and tear has taken away the joy of the new, you are lost; you stand on nothing solid. You don't know who you are, do you? Is it as if you are nothing?" Hearing the whisper I reach for my credit card and find a rebound.

In late modernity, when identity is based on the thinness of consumption and intimacy, your very self-definition is confronted by its thinness, its proximity to nothingness. The very fact that you can have your identity stolen in our world shows how thin and easily destroyed identity can be; and when identity is destroyed in our time, it is as if you don't exist, for there is no other meaning, authority, or community of belonging to hold you without question.

MY BODY AS MY IDENTITY

When consumption and intimacy are the driving forces of identity, then the body (your individual body) becomes the location and end for creating your (many) self-definitions. The body, then, becomes the location to form identity; the style of our bodies becomes how we broadcast our self-definition. I use my body to hang my consumptions on, and I use my consumption to attract intimacy to my body. It is not the time and space of my traditional community or the time and space of my work and love that set the terms for my identity; rather it is only the style of my body, it is only what my body possesses and who is attracted to it that matters in my self-identity. I may be the smartest person in the class, the spouse of a caring wife, with an important job, but the looks I get from strangers (whether good or bad) seem to have more power in defining me, for their glances provide commentary on my body.

When my body is the location to formulate identity through consumption and intimacy, I'm forced to beat my body; I'm forced to mold it in a way that makes it a commodity that others will want to possess, that will get the glances I desire, that others will want intimacy with. Or I give into the nothingness of this pursuit and let myself go, choosing obesity over the constant strain of body modification. Both options provide self-definition and both play a tune of nothingness. One strums that my body and its molding is all that there is so I will work like hell to beat back death by making meaning and finding belonging through definition of my body, fearing (with the fear of death) that if my body is no longer attractive it is as though I've died. The other hums a dirge of defeat, urging me to give myself over to death, for my body will never be something worthy of consumption, never be a lodging for intimacy. "Let death take me," it hums.

My identity belongs to my body; it broadcasts who I am. I often serve the monster by forcing my body to conform to my wishes for it. If I perceive myself as fat, I must obey the monster by starving myself so that I might have a self-definition I'm proud of. And even if it isn't this dire, even if I avoid starving myself or piercing my flesh to broadcast my identity, I still (and I really mean *I*) feel the need to use my body to present my identity. I wear clothes I hope communicate to my students that I'm hip so that I might have an identity as a relevant teacher. I've even (and here is an embarrassing confession) thought about buying the Perfect Pushup (you know, calling after the infomercial to order that gadget designed by Navy SEALs that scientifically generates the perfect push-up and therefore gives you chiseled biceps and chest), hoping that a little definition of my body will give me a more dynamic self-presentation and in turn self-definition.[3]

THE DEATH OF IDENTITY

When identity is bound in the style of the body it has opened itself up to nothingness, for there is nothing constant about who I am other than my constant search for things to buy for my body and people to be intimate with it. My identity then can easily slip away from me, leaving me alone, leaving me without any knowledge of who I am and where I belong. Our bodies are *always* changing; they are always moving toward atrophy—not even a truckload of Botox can stop it. In the irony of the monster, the more unconsciously we fight against death through our bodies, the more we serve it. When identity is as thin as new jeans, anxiety rushes to the surface. For if we fail to keep up, it can feel like we fail to exist.

Tyler Durden, the Brad Pitt alter ego of Edward Norton in *Fight Club*, sums up much of this. The Norton character feels himself stuck, unable to define who he is, unable to find meaning and community (he makes up illness and addictions to visit Twelve Step programs because he feels so cut loose). Feeling unbound to anything and unable to sleep due to his depression, unbeknownst to his psyche he takes on an altogether new identity (Tyler) and fails to recognize that these two self-definitions exist in one person. Tyler becomes everything Norton's charter wishes he could be. Abandoning work and love, seeing the flaws in consumption and intimacy, they decide to find what is real by literally beating their bodies, by starting a fight club. When they do, hordes of people who feel like Norton join. At the beginning of one meeting Tyler gives the manifesto of the club, a manifesto born from the very thinness of identity:

> Man, I see in Fight Club some of the strongest and smartest men that ever lived. I see all this potential and I see it squandered. An entire generation pumping gas, waiting tables, slaves with white collars. Advertising has us chasing cars and clothes, working jobs we hate so we can buy more s**t we don't need. We are the middle

children of history, man. No purpose or place. We have no Great War, no Great Depression. Our Great War is a spiritual war; our Great Depression is our lives. We've all been raised on television to believe that one day we would all be millionaires and movie gods and rock stars, but we won't. We're slowly learning that fact and we're very very pissed off.

When we recognize the thinness of identity and anxiety rushes in, the monster has grabbed us and we become angry or depressed, hating others or ourselves.

THE CHURCH AND THIN IDENTITY

And so here stands the church, busy with many things, busy pushing for new worship styles, new outreach forms, new models of youth ministry, better curriculum, and more impressive buildings. Here is the church presenting itself as a place able to be consumed, a place that offers intimacy. The church is fighting for its own self-definition, spilling ink and vomiting words on its own identity ("The church is like . . .", "the church needs to be . . ."). I have been in a number of churches where the sermon becomes a commercial for what the church is doing and what the church is about.

But as the church continues to talk about who or what it is and needs to be in the future, it fails to recognize that many of us feel ourselves confronted by a more insistently haunting question; we are asking from the core of our being, in nearness to the monster, "Who am I?" And the church often only stutters out broken phrases about its own identity. It offers nothing to us—no assistance, no imagination—in helping us understand ourselves alongside the nothingness of death and the work of the monster all around us. We feel as if we are drowning without answers. When intimacy has lost its electricity and our things are outdated, we know we have little understanding of who we are. And the church seems silent, too busy with itself—too busy ignoring the vicious stare of the monster through its veil of positivity—speaking of its own identity so that the church need not face the reality that death surrounds it. It need not see that in the end worship style, youth ministry programs, and new education wings are meaningless.

The church can revive, revitalize, and reemerge all it wants, but until it has something to say to this question, "Who am I?" it has not left the mountain top of self-obsession to enter the valley of despair, the valley where identity is destroyed in the harsh aftertaste of consumption and the brokenness of lost intimacy. There are so many voices that provide answers to the question "Who am I?" Every ad, commercial, or glance seems to be providing an answer: "you are *this* if you wear that . . . ", "you are *that* if you are with him." But there are few places where we are welcomed when we have been crushed by the lies of consumerism or the loss of intimacy, places to go to seek answers to who we are in the despair of loss. The church can revive, revitalize, or reemerge all it wants, but until it faces death it is only playing house.

But the church can only be this place of welcome for those crushed if it stops asking, Who are we as the church? and begins asking, Who is this God that enters death? The primary question for our ministries is not, What is the church? But, who is God for us and how can the church witness to this God? For when we ask this question we are confronted with death. We see a God who does not fear the monster, but suffers the monster, taking death unto God's very self in the crucified Christ.

Nietzsche was right: there is more than a little nothingness in our modern world, a nothingness late modernity has unveiled even further. "The Nietzschean concept [of nihilism] corresponds most closely to this fluid and anchorless sense of reality" many of us feel.[4] In these last four chapters we have seen that the monster is loose in our world. We have seen that despair and nothingness are ever close. Our deepest questions reveal this. We are asking, "Is there any meaning?" "Who says?" "Who do I belong to?" and "Who am I?" These questions cannot be answered by the form or perspective of the church; they can only be answered by turning to contemplate a God who enters death and despair for the sake of life. In the midst of the darkness and confusion of our questions we must seek a God who enters darkness, who makes our questions of despair God's very residence.

REFLECTING ON THE STORY OF SCRIPTURE

Jacob

Isaac was born from the despair of a dead womb; his boys would come into the world in conflict, the younger of the twins, Jacob, holding the heel of the older, Esau. Their names summed them up. Esau was strong, hairy, and manly. Jacob was a heel, a trickster, a con man. His brother was built like a linebacker, a man to build a nation on, Jacob in his shadow was as slimy as Eddie Haskell. With some help from his mother the "heel" pulled the greatest con, tricking his blind father, the promise himself, Isaac, for his blessing, a blessing supposed to be given to the older Esau. Like all good con men, by the time Esau could see that he had been had, the "heel" was gone.

Using his charlatan ways Jacob over the years acquired a great amount of stuff that seemed to help him deal with the fact that he was just the "heel." But now it was time to meet his brother from whom he had been running, knowing that when they meet his brother will likely kill him. When there is no avoiding it, and the confrontation must happen, like the schemer that he is he first sends cattle (in other words, he sends suitcases of cash), but fearing that wouldn't work he sends his children and wives, hoping they will assuage Esau's rage.

Now alone, the "heel" is met by a man and in a repeating of the wrestling that would bring him into the world, he would wrestle with this other, this masked man. They would wrestle all night. As the darkness breaks the masked man touches Jacob's hip, putting it out of joint, revealing that he is more than an ordinary man, that he is supernatural. Holding on, Jacob, who is more of runner than a fighter, nevertheless pleads for a blessing. Asking for his name, Jacob tells him, "I am Jacob, the 'heel,' the con man." "No," the angel says, "you are now given a new identity for you have wrestled with God. You are Israel." The "heel" is made into the continuation of the promise of his father, the despair borne in the "heel," the impossibility of "heel" has been taken up by God, wrestled, and made into the promise. The impossible has happened; the "heel" has become the promise. He will continue to limp as a sign that he has wrestled with God in despair, but in his wrestling despair he has been blessed; he has become the promise.

DISCUSSION QUESTIONS

- *Jacob receives a new identity in his wrestling with God. How have you wrestled with God and how has it changed you?*

- *In this chapter we saw that identity is much more fluid than it was in the past. How do you see this in your context? What issues does this raise for you?*

- *How can your congregation be a place where people are invited to wrestle with God, to make their wrestling their very identity?*

PART TWO

I WAS IN FIFTH GRADE, eleven years old, when the monster appeared and struck Denny dead.

He was about the same age as I was when sickness and a rigid and demanding father unveiled the nearness of the monster to him.

I was standing right behind Denny doing the safest, most benignly American activity possible, watching a local neighborhood championship Little League Baseball game. Right in the middle of the nostalgic glow of childhood, right in the middle of our safe suburban neighborhood—right there, right then, with Jared, Denny's son, on deck—the monster struck.

Martin Luther, now a little older, was just walking, making his way across his village, school and his rigid father on his mind. It was right there, right in the middle of normal life, that the monster threatened him again. As he walked the same path he had taken hundreds of times, the sky changed and lightning struck, just missing him. As the thunder clapped and the ground shook with the impact of the lightning, he screamed out for the saints to help him.

As the ambulance rushed to Denny, as the sirens vibrated in my ears, I was struck speechless with fear.

Both of us made deals with God. Luther promised that if he could make it through the field and find himself safe from the lightning he would enter the monastery. I promised that I would follow Jesus and really devote my life to him by listening to Christian music, wearing Christian T-shirts, and being the best of boys. We had seen the monster and could not face it. We had seen the monster and needed protection; we needed Christianity to hide us from the disorienting reality that the monster of death was in world.

Both of us were devoted to fulfilling our promises. I prayed daily, went to all the youth ministry activities I could, never drank alcohol, and told my friends about Jesus. Luther fasted, prayed for hours, slept on a hard bed, and confessed his sins incessantly. But the more he did, the more the monster would laugh, forcing him to question if he was doing it right and doing enough. So he upped the ante, praying more, fasting longer, beating his body into submission. He wanted so badly to please God and keep the monster of death away. But it seemed the more he did the more he heard the cackle of the monster and the more death was not extracted from him but curled up next to him, putting its ice cold body on his and whispering, "It's meaningless—death is coming for you." It was as if the monster laughed at his actions, pushing him into great doubt and depression. It appeared, to Luther's anguish, that *doing more* and *trying harder* were like steroids for the monster, for all this doing and trying was shown to be only a flimsy shelter; and the monster grew in power as Luther tried obsessively to hide from death. He had survived the lightning, but nevertheless death was ever close. This God who saved him seemed silent and absent compared to the accusations of the monster.

THE THEOLOGICAL BREAKTHROUGH

But then it occurred—Luther's theological insight that forever changed the church, a theological insight that few of us, even those who trace our heritage back to him, have yet to truly confront. Up against death and despair, Luther asked the greatest nihilistic question that could possibly be mustered in his time, centuries before Nietzsche. In a time when the world was organized around providence, a world where God brought rain and ordained some to rule, in a world where God was at the center of everything, where it was God who both brought and saved people from lightning, Luther asked the ultimate question, the question at the heart of nothingness. With extreme bravery in the swirl of despair, he asked, "What if this God, this God I have tried and tried to please, what if this God is *not* good, for this God cannot protect me from the darkness of the monster?"

It was from this question, from bringing this question into his reading of Paul, that the great theological insight of the Reformation occurred: that we are justified by faith through grace alone. The great insight is that it is not what *we* do that matters but what *God* has done for us.

WHAT WE MISS IN LUTHER'S BREAKTHROUGH

Those of us in Protestantism still revel in how such a theological assertion reformed the church, freeing it from its bureaucratic corruption to seek authentic community with God and each other. But too often we stop here. We see Luther's great insight that it is by grace and not works that we are saved, but we miss that this insight was discovered through desperate wrestling with death and nothingness. The great breakthrough of the Reformation, the great reforming of the church (that we are still trying to live into) was born through the facing of death, through the searching for a God of love by placing oneself eye-to-eye with the monster. We don't seem to care about the wrestling, only its outcome, which pushes us into a distortion of the church and Christianity, and therefore seeing Luther as our hero.

But when we do, we have a problem, because heroes in all their forms seem to be those that transcend the monster of death. The hero is the one that has power over death, the one that lives and acts beyond death. But Luther was no transcender; in many ways he was an anti-hero, a pathetic, depressed, and overindulgent monk. He deserves no T-shirts with pictures of his face on them. He is no super-star; he is a deep sufferer, weak in so many ways. His whole life he would battle with death, with what he called his *Anfechtungen*. His great despair was that he could not shake death, could not climb into a pretend clubhouse of opti-mism. He was no transcendent hero who possessed the power to rise above death; he knew death, he knew its enveloping power, and he knew its promises of nothing-ness (even after his great theological breakthrough). He had days and weeks where the monster pinned him to his bed, where he was caught only in the suction of the pull of nothingness.

It was in the midst of despondency, up against death, that Luther discovered that the God he found in the despair of his monastic cell and in the pages of the Pauline Epistles was also no heroic transcendent one. For Paul says, "For I decided to know nothing among you except Jesus Christ and him crucified. And I was with you in weakness and in much fear and trembling" (1 Cor. 2:2-3 RSV). What Luther discovered, which we too often hide from, is the theological and existential discovery that God is crucified, that the monster takes God, that death and separation destroy God. And this is not to be celebrated, but despaired. Just like Paul, we are in much fear and trembling. For Luther, like Nietzsche, God is dead. But unlike Nietzsche, Luther is more radical, for it is not our conceptions of God that are dead, but God in Godself. For Luther, God is dead, dead on a cross by choice. The monster has taken God (for God desires to be so with us in the real world, a world where death is our destiny, that God too takes on this destiny).

This more radical assertion allows Luther to go where Nietzsche cannot. For Nietzsche there is only death, but for Luther salvation is born in death. Light comes only through darkness, for God is found first on the cross, overcome by death. "For it is the God who said, 'Let light shine out of darkness,' who has shone in our hearts to give the light of the knowledge of the glory of God in the face of Christ" (2 Cor. 4:6).

A STARTING POINT: YOUR DESPAIR

Therefore, Luther's starting point for his theology, a starting point that has somehow gotten lost in modernity's centuries of obsession with progress, is that the God of Jesus Christ is known in the despair of death. It is when we are up against death, when we find ourselves in despair, that the God of cross is near to us. It is through suffering and despair that God is made known to us, for God is found on the cross. Luther's starting point is that only those who despair will have eyes to see the God who makes Godself known in the crucified Christ.

This not a celebration of masochism for Luther—he has already tried that. He has beaten his body, gone without sleep, and starved himself to please God. Rather, this idea that God meets us in despair and death is freedom, for it isn't what we do (even to the extent of making ourselves suffer) that matters, only the willingness to admit our frailty, to see that death is our destiny and that no matter what we do we cannot escape it. It is not in masochism but in living honestly next to (at least in our time) the death of meaning, authority, belonging, and identity that we will discover the paradox that God is near in death, that out of despair we find life.[1] We have tried to find God in other places, but God, according to Luther, is found first on a cross, beaten and dead, not as a masochist but as bearer of what is, a God who takes on our destiny of death in all its forms.

We can see this clearly in Luther's *Heidelberg Disputation*, a document written to defend his theological breakthrough. In the first dozen theses Luther speaks of impossibility: the impossibility of pleasing God, of escaping evil, and of escaping the law of death.[2] He has tried (and tried hard) to please God, to find God in his own action by moving himself away from death. But away from death there is no God, Luther believes. In thesis 18 he makes his turn toward theological construction.[3] "It is certain" Luther states, "that [people] must utterly *despair* of [their] own ability before [they are] prepared to receive the grace of Christ." This doesn't mean that people must think that they "suck," pushing themselves into self-loathing, necessarily, but they must recognize that the monster will win, that they are helpless in the face of death, that death and all his friends are always and unrelentingly closing in on us. Nothing we do will stop it. It is not that you "suck." It is that you are surrounded, you are helpless; the monster will prevail.

A SECRET

But there is a great secret here, a secret that the world caught up in avoiding death cannot slow itself down to see, a secret that calls the church deeply into a reality of death. It is a secret that asserts that if we will despair, if we will be willing to face death, if we will bear reality, we will discover an amazing paradox, an amazing reality: that the God of life through the Incarnation, Crucifixion, and Resurrection has made death and despair the very location of God's being. Douglas John Hall states: "Luther's Christ forever returns to his cross, to his grave, to hell, in order to be 'with us.' He can be for us only insofar as he is with us."[4] God is found in the despair of the cross. God is found in our many deaths, bringing possibility out of nothingness.[5]

It is *not* that creation itself is not wonderful and beautiful; it is not that love of children and friends is hollow. Rather, it is admitting that these things (and so many more) are so full and so wonderful that it is deeply disturbing to fathom how they can so quickly and so suddenly disappear. Despair is the realization that there will be a day that my son and daughter will be without me, or more correctly, I will be without them. Suffering is the inability to hold on to these beautiful moments that so quickly disappear. It is not distaste for life that causes us despair. It is true that life can be vicious, but it is love for life that causes us great pain, for nothingness is always so close in joy, happiness, and fulfillment. The monster, even in moments of great fullness, promises that nothingness is on its way.[6]

The reformation of the church, then, does not start with ideas and actions alone. We have too often believed that if we could just get a handle on postmodern theory or learn a handful of new practices we could change our churches. It doesn't even start with simply a theological theoretical insight. Rather, it starts with the bravery to enter into the despair of death, with the audacity to seek the God of life in the deaths in our world and in ourselves. And as we have seen in Part One, there are many deaths in our world that deeply touch our lives. Too often we have asked, "What should we do?" Or, "How should we think about this?" But the real question, the question that is sought in the *Heidelberg Disputation* is, Who is this God? Who is this God and where does this God encounter us? Luther answered that this God is the crucified one and this God encounters us in death and despair, for this God has borne the full reality of annihilation. It cannot be happiness or wholeness where God encounters us. This may be a result of God's encounter, but it cannot be the location. For if happiness and wholeness is the location of God's encounter then only those who can be happy and whole can know and be with God. Only those who have denied the reality of living can claim to have encountered God. But God is not made known first in glory, but in brokenness, the brokenness of the body of Jesus.

THE CHURCH AS THE
COMMUNITY OF DESPAIR

Christianity is faith in a God who enters death, who is overcome by the monster so that the monster might be overcome. The church then is the community of despair, the community that enters deeply into the world for the sake of

shared despair, for the sake of seeking God in the nothingness that the monster brings. The church is the community
that enters into despair as celebration and joy, for entering
into the despair of ourselves and our world we confess we
are encountering God. In so doing we are *not* discovering
the answer to our many questions of yearning, confusion,
and suffering, but rather the very presence of God in these
broken places. This is worth celebration and worship!

It may be that the church has heard the theological
insight of the early Reformation ("You are saved by grace
alone"), but has yet to mold itself as the people of the crucified one, the people who seek God in death, people who,
though they fear, are not paralyzed by death but invite all
people suffering death, yearning, and brokenness to share
in the community of those who face darkness for the sake
of the light of God.

If this is true, if Luther is right, then it is not what you do
or even what you think that makes you a Christian; it is
your desire to seek God in broken places, up against the
monster. To be a Christian is to be one who knows impossibility in your own being and in our world, and to seek God
in the midst of impossibility, not around or outside it. If
Luther is right, then you cannot lead a faith community if
you cannot face darkness; you cannot even be a Christian
unless you are willing to enter into death, for Christians are
those who follow Jesus Christ, and where Jesus Christ can
be found is in places of nothingness, bearing nothingness
for the sake of new possibility. It is no wonder that we have
seen Luther's theological breakthrough (justification by
faith alone) outside his own deeply lived theological assertion (God meets us in despair). Modernity has asked us to
be positive, to seek a religion that avoids such scary things,
for if we dared contemplate these things we would see that
modernity itself is a lie. But now in late modernity, up
against the many deaths and despairs that we discussed in
Part One, it may be time to return to the core of Luther's
lived theology—that God is near in suffering, brokenness,

and yearning, that God is encountered on the cross, that there is a promise in despair.

The church has no power in itself to bring forth possibility (it is God who brings forth new possibility); the church has only the call to enter despair with the promise that in so doing it will encounter the living crucified God who, through God's own beaten body, is working life and possibility out of death and impossibility. If the church seeks to be a place that can address the death of meaning, the death of authority, the death of belonging, and the death of identity, then it must be a place that seeks the crucified God, Jesus Christ, in these deaths. It must be a place that seeks to live through death.

Therefore, Part Two will explore a Christianity and Christian church that sees despair as promise, that seeks to encounter Jesus Christ in places of death, yearning, and brokenness.

As we move forward I have a warning. The next chapter (chapter 5) is the most technical chapter of the book; it is a chapter that delves deeply into the early Reformation theology of the cross. If you find yourself thinking, *I get this, I'm following this, but I want to see this perspective in conversation with discipleship, community, justice, and hope; I don't have time for the technical,* then skip ahead. Yet chapter 5 is important for driving deeper the point of this introduction and for seeing the cross and God's taking on of death as the central motif for discussing God's presence. So if you're up for it, hang in there.

CHAPTER FIVE

WILL DEATH EVER FALL IN LOVE?

The Cross

I T WAS ALREADY FIFTEEN MINUTES past his bedtime when he asked me the question. The question had its origins in the nightmares Owen had had months earlier. Back then, trying to comfort him in the midst of the fear, I had explained that though his nightmares seemed powerful and able to get him, they could not; they could not because Jesus had him. I explained that when Jesus went to the cross and overcame death with life, death was beaten. I showed Owen a picture of his baptism and explained that when he went under the water he was given over to death, but when he came out of the water he was given over to Jesus who brings life out of the dark waters of death. Though death was still powerfully in the world and could scare us with nightmares and trick us into doing bad things, it could not determine our destiny, for Jesus had swum deeply in the dark waters of death for the sake of bringing life out of them. So I explained that whenever he was scared of a nightmare he could say a little mantra I made up, "Death can't get me, because Jesus has got me."

Now, Owen was only three when I explained this to him (I agree it may have been a little much). But he seemed to get it. Seeing the newly white streaks in the chin hair of our black lab, Owen asked what they meant. When we explained that the white hair meant Kirby was getting older, Owen asked, "What happens then?" Pushing us to every next scenario, we finally explained that Kirby, our dog, will eventually die. Owen just shook his head and said, "I don't want that. I don't want death to have Kirby." Weeks later on a family walk Owen tripped, skinning his knee. As he fought back tears, we asked him if he was OK. Looking at us intensely and pointing to his red knee he said, "Yes, but death hurt me; death made me bleed."

So it was no surprise when he asked me this question. It was already past his bedtime and Owen was filled with many questions. So as I hurried to tuck him in, Owen asked, "Daddy, will death ever fall in love?" Recognizing that this was an important question, but also not sure if it was another tactic to stall his inevitable bedtime, I responded, "Yes, Owen, death will fall in love and when it does love will destroy death, and death will be no more. Now go to sleep. Good night." And I walked out.

But Owen had stumbled upon it. This question ("Will death ever fall in love?") was the most fundamental of all questions—the question, in many ways, that the whole universe rests upon. Is there an answer to death? Is love or death stronger? Will death ever not be? Will death itself ever be transformed? And how? These are the most essential of questions; the whole of existence is caught up in them. There is no one in the world who doesn't bump up against them. The church has spent way too much time giving answers that avoid this question, thinking it possesses some kind of truth to fight for, some kind of meaning, authority, belonging, and identity that can shield people from the reality of the monster of death. We have given our attention to other questions when the very questions of the universe, the very questions of our being, are lying in our laps. In quiet moments, in moments of great joy, in moments of great fear, in moments of great transition, where the present slips into the past, we can hear the question bubbling up from our very being, "Will death ever fall in love? Or is death, in its many faces, all there is?" Our very beings yearn for life and love, but there is so much death around us (lost jobs, lost love, deep fear, and brokenness), and even if we can avoid it all, we know that no one gets through this life alive. So will death ever fall in love? Is there something more than death? Is love able to conquer death?

LOVE BEYOND HALLMARK SENTIMENTALITY

Love is only able to conquer death if love goes through death. Love is only able to conquer death by dying. Or to say it another way, love is only love if it is found next to death, if it is found next to darkness, yearning, and brokenness.

Jerry is the kind of guy who never has a hard time getting a date but seems to have the hardest time finding the right girl, or at least the right girl who causes the relationship to last more then a few months. Jerry explains that he always breaks these off, not because he doesn't like the girls, but because they all seem to have baggage. He explains, "Once I know them for a few months they start telling me all this stuff, all this deep stuff, and I just find myself not wanting to go there."

It is hard for the consummate bachelor to finally commit to another, but not because he doesn't want to love her or even be with her. He cannot commit because he is not willing to face death; he is not willing to open his being to such an extent that it is vulnerable. He is not willing to have all the emptiness in him and in her revealed. Love does this; love exposes death, shakes it out from its hidden places. Jerry is afraid to love because love puts to death by revealing death; it puts to death that he can live without her, that he can live without love. He is not willing to love because love means sharing his own and her darkness; love exposes pain, yearning, and loss, and asks us to make pain, yearning, and loss the soil of our love. Jerry can't say "I love you" not because he is allergic to love, but to death. To love is to enter death. To love is to bind yourself so completely to another that their very being puts parts of yours to death. It is to open our beings to the ways the monster confronts them, to wrap our beings together in vulnerability to death. Love is born through death. Love is to be together through the storms of existence.

So to say that God is love is to say that God knows death. If the monster is in the world, if death takes four-year-olds in a cancer ward and fathers as they watch their sons play baseball, if death promises to take us, if we wrestle with it even now, then God can only love us if God meets us in death. And God must seek us in death, for God desires the love of relationship, because God honors relationship.[1]

To encounter God in the fullness of love is to encounter God alongside and through death. There is no other way. Love outside death is only sentimentality, a cheap illusion, only mutual denial-based affirmation. Love outside death is for Hallmark. I can't love my wife unless I'm willing to see and join her in those broken places of yearning, loss, and suffering that she knows. I can't love her if I refuse to see her alongside and through these places where the stench of death is real. God cannot be love unless God willingly enters death. God cannot be with us and for us unless God allows death to be wrapped around God's own being.[2]

The Incarnation, we confess, is God becoming human in the person of Jesus Christ. The Incarnation is God (God!) entering a world where death reigns. God becomes human in Jesus Christ, meaning that all that is true for humanity becomes true for God. No human being can escape the monster of death, so God must die. Incarnation leads to crucifixion. God now becoming human means God must die! The church worships a dead God—or better, a God who knows death by being overtaken by death for the sake of love.

It was this very reality that Paul held on to: "I choose to know only Christ and him crucified."[3] He refused to separate Christ and him crucified; to know Jesus is to know him through death, for to know him through death is to know him as the fullness of a God of love. There is no Christ without his cross, for without the cross there is no answer to the question, "Will death ever fall in love?" Without the cross there can be no love stronger than death, for God has not entered our reality; God cannot be with us unless God is with us in death, for death is our ultimate destiny. Without the cross Christianity cannot face death and therefore can only be in the business of delusional, sentimental Hallmark positivity. Christianity, for Paul, is at its very core about a God who enters death. In a world that knows death (as we saw in Part One), hyperpositivity has no correlation with reality; the church is meaningless because it cannot face reality. It cannot face death. Instead, as we see in Paul, the church should be the community that proclaims to the world that God knows death by loving the world—by entering the world's many deaths through the cross of Christ.

SEEKING ANSWERS TO OUR QUESTION

It was this very Pauline emphasis that lead to Luther's great breakthrough. The reformation of the church rested on a deeply theological imagination that we have yet to let influence how we understand and act as the church. We are justified by faith alone, because for Luther God, in God's love, has entered into death. This is what Luther called his theology of the cross. It is bankrupt, Luther believed, to look for God in the good things we do. It is worthless to look for God in a power-hungry church. It is confusing to seek God in the created order. God is revealed, Luther believed, in the cross.[4] To know God, to encounter God, is to recognize God in the death on the cross. God appears to us first and foremost in the dead peasant from Nazareth we call the Christ.

Owen's question, "Will death ever fall in love?" can only be answered by contemplating the event of this dead peasant, who is called Lord. Nature, although beautiful and God's good creation, has no answer—it is mute. Creation may possess beauty, but even its beauty must bow to death; nature operates in cycles, laws, and rhythms, not from love. By itself, nature tells us that death will never "fall in love," for cycles and rhythms of birth to death can never be overcome. We may be able to enjoy the ecstasy of the moment, say overlooking the Grand Canyon, but the moment must die (and if you fall over the edge and tumble down into the canyon, the moment becomes hell; what was beautiful is now torture).

The church in its bureaucratic and even traditional functions has no answers, for as a social organization it seeks its own life; it cannot tell whether "death will fall in love" because it must fight for enough power to continue to exist in society. It must use its worship services, buildings, and programs not to seek God in death and despair but rather as ways to maintain the church's (rapidly slimming) societal power. Love cannot be found when people or institutions grab for power, for love gives of itself. Love is found where people choose weakness over power so that they might be together.

Our own good works cannot answer, "Will death ever fall in love?" because our own good works, our own pursuits of holiness, lead us into ourselves, and within ourselves there is only death. Love is found outside of us, when we open our deaths to others and God. Love exists between others, not within an individual. Therefore, God does not meet us in the natural order, in power, or in individual holiness, but in lowliness, weakness, and suffering; for God desires to be with and for us. Out of great love, God chooses to be found in places of suffering and despair; God chooses to be found on the cross. Because it is God on the cross, because it is God who is crucified, suffering and despair become the location of God's very presence. For when God meets us in suffering and despair, God meets us in love. Luther wants us first to see God on the cross, and the cross can be nothing other than death; so for Luther God is found in death. God is found in despair.

DEATH ISN'T GOOD!

Luther does not think that suffering and death are good. There have been groups throughout history, as well as youth subcultures today, that essentially worship death. This is not Luther's point. Death, suffering, and brokenness are not good; they are only bad, only and fully annihilation. Luther is not after the worship of nothingness, but after the God who is made known in love by bearing nothingness. Because God has entered into death, God is found with those suffering death. God is found in the midst of a fifth grader's terror, standing with bat in hand and oversized batting helmet covering his shocked eyes as his lifeless father is hurried into an ambulance. God seeks to love us not around or outside but within our brokenness, bringing the hope of healing by sharing in our despair. The God of the cross is a God who makes Godself known in backward ways, in the opposite, as Luther would say.[5] It is not in power, advancement, or order that God meets us. In a world where the monster is roaming this would only quench his bloodthirsty cravings; rather, God is found in suffering next to death, in the embrace of those yearning for love and communion. This is where God is found (1 Cor. 1:18-19)!

In a world where meaning, authority, belonging, and identity are dissolving, showing the nearness of death all around us, it may be that hope is found through death; for when death is shared it is the fullness of love, the love of a crucified God. *Because God encounters us in death for love, it may be that we discover meaning in love that shares suffering, authority in the one who chooses weakness over power, belonging in the community that seeks God in despair, and identity as those broken and yet made whole through the brokenness of our Lord.*

It is only from the cross on the godforsaken hill of death outside of Jerusalem that we can begin to answer Owen's question, "Will death ever fall in love?" We too often assume that the cross was some kind of mechanical operation, some task that needed to be undertaken so that we might be forgiven and therefore need not earn our salvation, but this has little directly to do with love. I have heard handfuls of students preach sermons where the cross is simply an operation, a tool, that earns something, achieves something, and has nothing to do with the heart of God, with Love.

This perspective too easily becomes only monotone, dull statements without encountering the question, "Will death ever fall in love?" But the cross is where God battles the monster, where God confronts nothingness. And God must battle the monster not with the weapons of power and force, for that would only feed the monster of death and could lead to violence and oppression. Rather, God overcomes the monster by suffering the monster; God overcomes death by being overtaken by death. God overcomes the monster of death not with power and force but with weakness and suffering. Any other strategy would only feed death. Only love can overcome the monster, because only love is willing to become weak. Only love is willing to confront the monster with weakness.

THE DEATH OF THE TRINITY

On the cross God takes death into God's very history; God dies and death becomes part of God.

Jürgen Moltmann has captured this idea in great depth.[6] Moltmann argues that in the Crucifixion the Trinity itself is ripped apart by death. The Son is lost to the monster, sliding into nothingness, given over to death. And the Father is thrust into the heartache of loss; the beloved Son is ripped from the Father's hands, forsaken to death. God the Father knows loss and yearning, while God the Son knows the fear and abandonment of slipping into the void. The Crucifixion is a great agony not just for the disciples but for God in Godself. Because of the Love of Father to Son and Son to Father, the Love that *all* other loves mirror, the cross brings death into the very being of God. Within the inner life of the Trinity is the knowledge and experience of death; now death is inextricable from the being of God, for God has gone through it. Like a parent whose being is molded by the disability of his child, a parent who can no longer be the same now that his child is in the world as she is, God and death are inextricable. For God has experienced the fullness of nothingness. God knows death from the inside.[7]

But then here is the answer to my three-year-old's question; here is the answer to Owen's "Will death ever fall in love?" Because God has taken death so deeply into God's very being for the sake of love, God works life out of death; God brings possibility out of nothingness. In the lavish Love of God—a Love so deep, rich, and mysterious—in a Love so strong that it can bring being out of nonbeing, in such Love shared between Father and Son, God places death. In the cross death is placed between the Love of Father and Son. Death separates all loves, and Love shared in the Trinity is no different: it is split by death. But the Love of Father to Son is the very origin of love; it is love's source.

Death now located between the Father and the Son comes under the wonder of Love, and in this Love (this Love that is able to bring being out of nonbeing), death is broken. It is still death, but its power to separate is broken, for the Resurrection gives the Son back to the Father to never again be separated. Now through God's Love, from arid, dry, and ascetic death springs life. Death has been changed: it now exists between Father and Son forever; it has become part of God's story, of the Love story of the Father and the Son. Death might (and does) deceive us that it can separate. It may fool us into giving it power to determine our existence, but now existing between the Father and Son, it has no such force; between Father and Son, it is God who determines our destiny in Love.[8] Death bound between Father and Son means that those who experience death are taken into the compassionate Love of God; though they die or feel death's many stings, they are embraced in the Love of Father to Son. Those who suffer, suffer with God; they never suffer alone, but between the Love of Father and Son.[9] *It then is in despair, in facing the reality of death honestly, that we are encountered concretely by God; for death exists between the Love of Father to Son.*

Now, true life and true possibility are born from the yearning, loss, and brokenness of death; for yearning, loss, and brokenness are taken into Love. To love another is to know them through their deaths. It is to know them in yearning and despair, for to know them in their despair is to know them as loved by God in the frail naked beauty of their humanity, a humanity God, through Jesus, has taken unto Godself as the fullness of God's love for the world through death.

Seeking God in death is true life because it has gone through death and now death can no longer touch it. In the Resurrection God brings new life out of death. From the perspective of the Resurrection we see an all-new reality, a reality that is opposite of everything else—that is, we see that God works from death to life. Out of death comes life, therefore destroying death, all for the purposes of love. God puts death to death in the death of Godself. God is forsaken to Godself (Son to Father) so that death can *no longer* separate and destroy us. God is abandoned to Godself so now those facing death, four-year-olds and baseball-watching fathers, might never again be abandoned. God is alone in death so that those facing all forms of death might not ever be alone again but might find, with the eyes of faith, the abandoned, forsaken, suffering God with and for them in their many experiences of death.

THE CHURCH, LIVING FROM DEATH TO LIFE

The church is the community that seeks to live from the new order—not from life to death, but from death to life. The church seeks to enter deeply into death (speaking of it, preaching about, and so on) because it knows that by bearing death life is born from it. The church has too often closed its eyes and tried to only be about life. I know a church where nine out of ten sermons are about self-help, about what we can do to have better marriages, to be better parents, to be closer to God. Each sermon seems to have a number of principles that promise success. But how many sermons speak to the truth most of us experience? How many sermons say something to the reality that we live more in failure than success, more in yearning than fulfillment?

I know of a preacher who sees it as her job to speak the truth from the pulpit, and the truth is not only the reality of God's love, but also our brokenness. Her sermons seek to drive into the rawest places of our existence, letting the biblical text speak to these bleeding places.

Yet when the church refuses to do ministry in these raw places, up against death, it has not only denied reality but also become a bland place, for it seeks to hold on to life without recognizing that it is only by bravely entering death that we can find life. The church should be a weird community in a world that hides from death. The church should be a community of people that talk about despair, that confront it, knowing that when they do God is present, working life out of experiences of death.

"Will death ever fall in love?" Yes! Yes, death has fallen in love! Death tried to hide in the shadows, but God entered the darkness, and death has been taken into the Love of Father to Son. Death has become part of the love story of the Father to Son, and so the Love of Father to Son, Son to Father, has consumed death. Death has fallen in love in the Love of the Father to Son, or to say it better, death has been consumed and therefore promises to be destroyed in the Love of the Trinity. Death still exists (and exists radically, as I have tried to argue), but death has now been taken and placed between the Love of Father and Son. One day it will be totally obliterated, but for now it exists tethered between the Love of Father and Son. The monster is still active, still separating, still killing, still seeking to destroy, still deceiving us that if we serve death we can escape death (this is the fullness of sin). But the monster is no longer free; the monster has been bound in love. The bars of Love of God for Godself cage the monster.[10] And it is out of this love of God for Godself (as Father and Son) that God takes all death into Godself, making God present in death and despair. God hollows out the power of death by giving Godself over to death, making death, suffering, and despair the place where God promises to be present. God consumes death in God's own death, making death the place to encounter God. In the backwardness of the gospel we see that love is at its fullest when it is found in death; we see that death is broken when others in relationship (as witness to God's relationship as Father and Son) share in our despair. This is what we yearn for most: we yearn for others to know us not outside our fears, brokenness, doubts, and yearnings, but within them.

THE CRITERIA TO BELONG TO THE CHURCH

The church is open to all people who are willing (in time) to open their deaths up to others. This is the criteria to belong to the church! Only those who know some kind of loss, yearning, and brokenness can be members in the community of the crucified Christ. The church can *never* be the community of perfect, trouble-free people; the church cannot be a club of the moral elite. If the church is a church of the cross, of the Love of Father and Son, it cannot be the community of denial in positivity. How is it that the church has gotten the reputation for being a people where you need to be perfect to be part of it? Where you have to have your crap together to belong? It is the utter opposite; only those who are willing to admit that their crap is in utter disarray (even if it looks orderly) are those who can be in, and lead, the church. At its beginning the church was considered, especially by the Roman elite, to be a distasteful community, a community that worshiped a dead Jewish peasant and invited lowly people not only to be part of it, but also to lead it.

The only criterion necessary to belong to the church is to know impossibility, suffering, yearning, brokenness, and failure. Only those who have had such experiences (which is everyone) are welcome. For it is only through our loss, yearning, and brokenness that the suffering God of Jesus Christ encounters us, and it is only through these experiences that we can really be in relationship with others. A church that cannot admit it is filled with those who suffer is a community that cannot share relationship with others, for relationships that are rich and transformative are relationships built through our shared loss, yearning, and brokenness, through despair. Just ask anyone in a Twelve Step program; their admission of powerlessness, of brokenness, becomes the fabric of their deep life together (as always-broken people).

THE PROMISE IN DESPAIR

So for Luther there is promise in our despair, for our yearning in despair is always taken up into the suffering Love of Father and Son. We partake in the very being of God as we seek God in our despair, for through the cross God has placed our despair at the very heart of God's life; God in love has taken on death and despair in Godself. This means that the church is the community that seeks death not as masochism, but as the way to love God and world. The church is the community that dwells deeply, both in its life and before the world, in the question, "Will death ever fall in love?"

It is amazing how little the church has dared to live with this question, how in many ways the church and our so-called doctrinally correct faith encourage us to deny or ignore this question. They encourage us to worry about things outside this question, to find ways to grow a church, ways to feel something spiritual, ways to be relevant. But this question, voiced by an overly reflective three-year-old, touches on the very essence of the questions that are wrapped tightly around our humanity and our faith. We know death is in the world, that death is within us, and from the core of our being we ask, What is stronger, love or death? Will death ever fall in love? Is there a love stronger than death? Most of the relationships we know are pocked by the heavy bombardment of death. Christianity has often made little difference to those in the world because the church too often has been unable to ask these questions with the world. It has not been brave enough to enter death, to see it and therefore witness to a love that is born from death. A Christianity that cannot, or refuses to, dwell on this question is a Christianity that has lost the cross.

The church of the cross is not a powerful community, but a weak one—a community that seeks to be in the world speaking of a reality that the world both is and is not aware of. The church is to speak of death and despair, it is to speak of the yearning that the world knows well, but it is also to speak of what the world does not know, the reality of a God who comes to us through the broken yearnings of our humanity.

I was taught after Benjamin's and Denny's deaths to seek a God who could shield me from this suffering. I was given a church that helped me deny it in spiritual pursuits. What I needed was for others to come beside me, even at four years old, and speak to me, as witnessed to in their person, of a God who comes near in our brokenness, fear, and loss. I needed to be pointed to a God on a cross, a God who would in love encourage me to be honest and to seek bravely to find God in my loss, not outside of it. The church serves the world by speaking of death and suffering. The ultimate power of death and suffering is that they render us mute (Jungel). Up against deep hurt, loss, yearning, and brokenness we are often thrust into silent loneliness. It is the church, from its theology of the cross, that "develops a language in which death is articulated and so given meaning. To speak of death is to defy it, to refuse its claim to paralyze."[11]

The church is not the place that makes those in the world suffer, causing them to despair, to see themselves as nothing but sinful worms. No, the church is the community that whispers that it knows what we so often seek to deny, it knows that we despair, that we yearn, that we fear. The church does not bring people to the foot of the cross, but only seeks to live so closely to people in love and confession that they are free to admit that it is true that the cross of death is before us all, that we (those in the church and those not) are broken and in need. It is then that the church proclaims in word and deed that in facing our despair *together* we are concretely encountering a crucified God who loves by sharing in our despair.

The church is the community that seeks God through the deaths in the world and in ourselves. Our preaching, teaching, outreach, and fellowship should all seek the crucified God—to explore death, to honestly bear it, to create a communal language that expresses it, and ultimately to wrestle with God to speak to us through our deepest yearning next to death. For it is here, in God's love, that promise is to be found.

The church often matters to so few people because the church has not been able to face reality. It has been the place of positive denial. But the church cannot be a place of love, the Love known through the crucified God, unless it is willing to abandon its hyperpositivity, abandon its need to be safe and clean, and instead seek to wrestle in the dirty pathos of human yearning. Our sermons, education times, board meetings, and coffee hours should be as deep as our yearning, as deep as the God who cries in the separation of Godself by death. As beautiful as a God who brings life and possibility out of death and impossibility. God moves through death; so should the church.

REFLECTING ON THE STORY OF SCRIPTURE

Mary

From the closed, dead womb would come Isaac and the continuation of the promise. But there would be no people, no nation Abraham was promised until they were freed from the despair of slavery in the womb of Egypt. Now out of the impossibility of another womb *the* promise, salvation, God in God's fullness, is made known. It is now through the impossibility of a virgin womb of the most insignificant of teenage girls that God would break into the world. Out of the despair of Galilee (a place from which nothing good comes), from the womb of an unmarried little girl, living in the oppressive shadow of Rome, the Messiah is born. And born not in glory, but in the bed of animals, right next to stench and breath, in the despair of a pregnant mother with nowhere to lay her head. A forgettable girl, a girl in a male-dominated society, a shamefully pregnant unwed girl, would be the bearer of God. From her despair comes the promise.

And she would not be the only one; there were other women of despair, like the other Mary, Mary of Magdalene, who would become the greatest of Jesus' disciples. There were those who first witnessed him alive on Easter morning, who from their despair and hopelessness at having lost him to death encounter him living. They were those who from their despairing situations before his death were able to see that he was the one. They could see that though he was born in the despair of poverty and lived in the despair of Galilee, and though he died the death of the despised and insignificant, the criminal and the depraved, he was the very promise, the promise born from the impossibility of the virgin womb of the peasant girl.

DISCUSSION QUESTIONS

- *Think about the birth of Jesus for a moment. What do you find the most surprising elements of the story? Where do you most clearly see despair?*

- *What do you find the most surprising in this chapter? What do you find the most confusing?*

- *Do you think our sermons, education programs, and coffee hours are as deep as our yearning? How could they be?*

CHAPTER SIX

THIS IS NO PEP RALLY; THIS IS AN ACTUALITY

Discipleship through Death

I ABRUPTLY LEFT OWEN that night with my answer that death would indeed fall in love and when it did, it would destroy death. But apparently my swift exit didn't end his deep contemplation about this question. As a matter of fact it seemed that my answer opened up another question for him. The next day, after lunch, Owen was playing with his *Star Wars* guys. As he was intently making them jump and talk, he stopped and turned to my wife and asked, "Mommy, will death ever fall in love?" Taken aback by the question, she answered, "I don't know, Owen; I'm not sure I understand." Owen continued, ignoring her plea for clarification, with his forehead and eyes pinched with intensity, "Daddy said that one day death will fall in love and when it does love will destroy death." "Oh," my wife responded, trying to imagine what we could have possibly been talking about. Owen then continued, his eyes opening wide as if to release the deep question that had been forming in the core of his heart for a day, "But, Mommy, that scares me, because I love you! Will I be destroyed?"

Three-year-old Owen had stumbled upon it once more. If love promises to destroy death, if even now love is found next to death, what does that mean for me? What does it mean if I love, if I follow the one who fully takes death into God's being to overcome it? Owen was right: love puts to death; for death, with its promise of separation, is love's enemy. But love mirrored in the Love of Father and Son overcomes its enemies by suffering its enemies. Love puts to death by embracing our loss, yearnings, and brokenness.

To love another is to be put to death. Owen was right: to love his mommy is to have parts of him destroyed. If he loves his mommy, he can never again live as if she doesn't matter. To love her he must allow those parts of him to die that would deny her in actions, attitudes, or inclinations of self-determination and self-preservation. For the sake of his love for her, he is called into death. To love her he must not only embrace her many deaths—her losses, yearnings, and brokenness—but he himself must face death; he must give up his own pursuits and desires so he might love her. He must die to himself. And of course the great wonder of this is that the more he is willing to do this, the more he is given back to himself in love. The more he is willing to enter her death and put those things in him that live in opposition to love to death, the more he is free, the more he is himself, for he was made for love. He was made to be in relationship with a God who loves Godself in the loving relationship of Father and Son.

LOVE PUTS TO DEATH

All those parts of us that live in opposition and contradiction to love must die, for God is Love. And this is discipleship: to follow Jesus Christ as he faces death for the sake of love. But the mystery of this is that *love* does this, not our effort. Love can't exist through the strain of individual striving; just ask all those girls in high school and college I tried to will toward loving me. I worked hard to get them to love me, but love does not exist in effort—rather, it exists next to death. To really love someone we must see that person; and that is to see this person through his or her deaths—through losses, yearnings, and brokenness. And so I must make also my own deaths vulnerably open. To be able to truly see another in this way means parts of me must face death. Love puts our penchants toward hate, isolation, and fear to death by absorbing them, by taking them into itself. This is why the cross, in its horror, is the most beautiful picture of love ever imagined.

The disciple then is the person who is open to others through the death of Jesus Christ. We can find love and solidarity with all people not because we are connected to them through similar religious commitment, agreed upon moralism, doctrinal fusion, or even religious practice. The disciple is open to all others because *all* others experience death. The follower of Jesus is called to all whom death touches (and no one can escape death). We are called this far because death is now located in the being of God. We go to others not to feel good, as though we have earned our discipleship stripes, but because to join others in death is to be near God, to participate in God's very ministry. The disciple of the crucified God is called to be with and for, as God is, all those who know implicitly or explicitly that death surrounds them. But this openness is not a kind of fluffy inclusivism. We are called as disciples to be open to people, not because it is nice or the right thing to do; no, we are called to be open to all people because *all* people through their loss, yearning, and brokenness are taken up in their deaths and placed between the Love of Father and Son. The disciple is open to all others through their brokenness and as the disciple opens his or her brokenness to others. We do this not because it works, but because we confess that this is where God is found. God is present when death is shared, when suffering is joined. We are open to others as our *identity*; we are those who love others through their loss, yearning, and brokenness, because God is found sharing and joining in their deaths, seeking to bring forth life.[1]

BUT WHAT ABOUT SIN?

I can hear it now, "This diminishes a doctrine of sin! What about sin?" As the book of Romans tells us, sin is death; that is why death always sucks—it is not good. Sin, then, is serving death. Sin is not ultimately the bad things we do; sin is the inclination toward serving death as the ultimate reality rather than serving the God who brings life out of death. Sin as the state of our being is the reality that we will die. We commit sins, do things that hurt others and stand in opposition to God, when we believe the deceptive lie of death itself. We sin when death whispers to us, "If you will serve me, I will keep you from dying," and we take up death's offer. We do things that hurt others because we are deceived into believing that if we sacrifice another to death, death will leave us alone. We sin because we find ourselves vulnerable to death, and to deny its reality we serve it. Therefore, sin can only be overcome through one who bears death, taking away its power by caging it within the Love of the Trinity. As Paul again reminds us, Jesus Christ has become sin, has become death, so that we might find life in the midst of death.[2] As disciples, then, we can only live lives in opposition to sin if we seek the God who is found in death. We can only live faithfully beyond death's deception if we take on death, if we face it and bear it.

THE DISCIPLE CARRIES HIS OR HER CROSS— WHAT'S THAT MEAN?

We often think, in our American individualist, do-it-yourself culture, that when Jesus calls his disciples to bear their crosses, he means to do things that are difficult, to choose a kind of life that is hard. We equate carrying our cross with raking the leaves or exercising, something that should be done, and in the end is good for us, but is nevertheless hard to do. Christians are those who live moral lives in a world where moral pursuits are not rewarded. So discipleship becomes not lying to get a better price, not drinking or having sex in high school, claiming that you go to church in a secular environment, or hanging a piece of Christian symbolism (a cross, a fish) in your work cubicle. This, we imagine, is carrying our cross; this is discipleship.

But this is *not* discipleship. This is benign at best, and obnoxious at worst, Christian moralism. To be a disciple is to be one who follows Jesus Christ. And Jesus Christ can only be found in death, working life and possibility out of its impossibility. The disciple, the follower of Jesus, is called into death. Dietrich Bonhoeffer opens his greatly loved book *The Cost of Discipleship* with the line, "When Jesus Christ calls a person, he calls them to come and die." We often read this, whether we'll admit it or not, as hyperbole, like a football coach who tells his team to go out there and kill the other team. His players roar with excitement, not because they anticipate really killing their opponents, but because the rhetoric has fueled them to play passionately. So we imagine that when Jesus says a disciple must take up her cross, or Bonhoeffer asserts that "Jesus calls his follows to come and die," it is only hyperbole meant to motivate us to live like we are Christians.

But this is *not* what Bonhoeffer means; he is following Luther (who is following Paul). Luther means that the disciple must enter death, must go to the cross; the disciple of the crucified Christ must be the person who enters into suffering and death. The disciple is known to the world not through his or her good morals or outward signs of commitment to his or her religion. No, the disciple, according to Luther and Bonhoeffer, is known by entering death with the world, is the one who seeks God by following Jesus Christ into the crevices of his or her own and the world's loss, yearning, and brokenness. The disciple is the one who in joy makes his or her home there. This is carrying the cross.

A NEW IDENTITY,
NEXT TO THE DEATH OF IDENTITY

In a world where identity is dying, as we saw in chapter 4, where it is becoming harder and harder to form a solid conception of ourselves, discipleship provides us an *identity*. It asserts that we, those who follow Jesus, are not better than those in the world (not even more moral or spiritual). Our distinct identity is in our openness. Our particularity as followers of Jesus is that we are those who look at suffering, those who grieve death, but those who nevertheless do not fear to make our life within brokenness, for we are the people who worship a crucified God. We are earthy people who bear reality, seeking God in the many deaths we face.

The disciple can only be a disciple by going through death—this is the identity of the Christian. Not because death is good! No, the disciple must enter the death within himself or herself and the world because that is where Jesus Christ is found. The disciple of the crucified Christ is the one who faces reality, who "calls a thing what is," as Luther would say. For Jesus is found dying, not simply so your sins can be forgiven, but so that your sins can be forgiven and you may find new life in the Love of Father to Son and the Son to the Father. There is only one route to find our lives, the narrow route of the disciple; it is the route that chooses death, that chooses to embrace and face the loss, yearning, and brokenness that cannot be extracted from us. It is a narrow path, not because it is only for the elect or enlightened; no, all can be Jesus' disciples. The only criterion to follow Jesus is to know death through loss, yearning, and brokenness, to not avoid it but enter it. It is a narrow path because few are brave enough to make their life in brokenness, few are brave enough to choose the weakness of love over the "strength" of power, few can recognize glory in the power to bear death. Discipleship is a narrow path because it calls for radical honesty—and this is costly.

THE HEART OF DISCIPLESHIP: HONESTY

This then is the shape of discipleship, a discipleship that can give us identity beyond the constant chasing of the new electricity of consumer goods and intimacy: the disciple is not the person who is holy, strong, or perfectly moral. The disciple is the person who is honest. Honesty is the heart of discipleship. The disciple is the person who admits that death is all around us, who seeks to search his or her own person and the world to see it honestly. The disciple is the person who is honest about loss, yearnings, and brokenness. This is Paul's desire in Romans 7:13 and following. The disciple is the one who seeks to see one's own person and the world "as it is." Honesty is the essential nature of discipleship because it is only when we admit our deaths that we can recognize and therefore follow the God who brings life out of death.

We must be honest about our deaths to follow Jesus Christ. Growth in discipleship isn't the ability to pray more, pray longer, fast, or avoid selfishness. Growth in discipleship is about being honest enough to see self and world, to recognize your vulnerability and yearning. Discipleship is seeking God in these honest places of barrenness, death, loss, and yearning. Praying, fasting, and avoiding selfishness help us honestly seek God in our loss, yearning, and brokenness. Discipleship, then, is the honesty to be truly human, to admit that we yearn for more, to open our eyes to reality, to wake up to despair and in great humility seek God. If it is in brokenness that God meets us then only those honest enough to admit their brokenness can follow Jesus Christ. As Kierkegaard has reminded us, faith in the crucified Christ is the willingness to dialogue with despair.

It appears the world has little time for the church, not because we are broken people, people seeking to be honest about our loss and yearning. The world has little time for the church because it sees it as a very dishonest place—a place where people like Ted Haggard rail against others as immoral to hide the deep (sinful or not) yearnings that live inside of them, a place where people do not see their duplicity, where people hide from reality in religion. The greatest missional direction the church might take is to remember that we are followers of the crucified God, a weak people who love not *outside* but *through* the honesty of our loss, yearning, and brokenness.[3]

During a visit to Solomon's Porch I was amazed by the honesty that flowed from the congregation, whether it came from people raising their hands after the sermon and articulating their doubt or in the heart-moving prayer requests spoken to the whole congregation. The church lives out of its desire to be disciples by first being honest.

The disciple is the one who loves God by finding God in the dead places in the world. The disciple is the one who becomes unholy by admitting his or her suffering, by being with those broken as he or she is broken, for from the perspective of the cross only those who are unholy, like the crucified Christ, can recognize God. (It was this very fact that transformed Saul into Paul: it was not until he saw the cross as God becoming unholy so that all might find communion with God that the cross was transformed from an offense to salvation.) The disciple is the one who enters death and suffering, for this is where the Lord is found, crucified.

NOW WAIT!

This sounds a little scary. This sounds like a disciple is someone who is masochistic. It could be misconstrued that I'm echoing the woman in the documentary *Jesus Camp* who explained that she admired Islamic fundamentalist terrorists not for their beliefs but for their devotion to their religion. She admired that they would blow up themselves and others for what they believed. This children's ministry director asserted that she wished the young people she worked with would commit (to be disciples!) in such a radical manner. As if such action proves (and I suppose it might) how deeply they believe and want to follow their religious convictions. But this is the last thing I am advocating! As a matter of fact, such a perspective can only be reached when we imagine that Jesus' call to carry our cross is to do hard things, to stand up against a culture that doesn't believe what we do. You can only get to this place if you refuse to be honest, seeing your brokenness in the brokenness of others. I assume if that is really what it means to follow Jesus, then the total commitment of violent death is the ultimate act.

But the disciple must go through death so that death is no longer determinative. The disciple goes through death, not to be annihilated, but to find possibility, to find life. Jesus is the way to life, but his way to life is through death. The disciple is not someone who believes vigorously, believes so much that he or she is willing to kill others or even himself or herself. This is misplaced worship; this is the worship not of the crucified God, but of death itself. A disciple is not determined by how much he or she believes, but only by how much he or she is willing to admit what is true—that we are all dying, that the monster is loose, that there are four-year-olds in cancer wards and little boys living without their fathers, that suffering and pain is real. But the disciple must admit more. The disciple proclaims, in his or her willingness to face death, that God is nevertheless present here. God in Jesus Christ is here in the middle of death, working for life. God is here in the middle of impossibility, promising that through God's own broken and now made-whole love, impossibility will someday give way to fulfilled possibility. The disciple is not the one who believes without doubt; the disciple is the one who doubts always, because the disciple is the one who stands honestly in reality, seeking God in death.

THE NEED FOR THE DISCIPLE TO DOUBT, THE NEED FOR THE CHURCH TO DOUBT

Seeking demands doubting. Seeking God in the midst of our loss, yearning, and brokenness, seeking God next to cancer-filled four-year-olds, demands that we doubt, that we push ourselves to think and feel, to question and wrestle with God in death. Discipleship is doubting while wrestling, for discipleship is facing despair. Doubt has no place in faith when faith brackets out suffering. But when suffering is central, when God is found on the cross, then we are called to follow God into the darkness of reality, and in the dark it is impossible not to doubt our perceptions, not to doubt our next step. But when discipleship is following the crucified God, then doubt is not a roadblock but the very lifeblood of faith, for it pushes us to honestly place our doubts before God and each other. Faith is the courage to dialogue with despair while trusting in the love of God.

The church is not a place of sure belief, but the community that trusts in a crucified God while it doubts. The church is the place that calls those in the world to come and doubt with it and within it (this is one of the most interesting things about Pete Rollins's Ikon community). The church is the community that places the doubts of the world before the God of love. It is the community that searches for God through our doubts, for our doubt is often not an intellectual reality (alone) but an existential one. Our doubts are wrapped around our fears and failures, around our brokenness and yearnings. Therefore, the church as the disciples of Jesus Christ calls all to come and doubt, to make their painful doubt known and in so doing seek God as we share life together.

Doubt can never be extracted from discipleship because the disciple is to orientate his or her life toward the future, toward a reality that is not here yet. The disciple is to face death while, through the power of the Spirit, bending his or her life toward a future where death will be no more. The great invitation of discipleship is to follow God into death. By living there we confess that death is bound within the Love of Father and Son, that there is a future that the Trinity itself is already living out, where death has no power, where death has been shattered in the overcoming of separation. The disciple stands with two feet in the world of despair, but he or she seeks to live not for this world that is passing away, this world that desires only death. Instead the disciple seeks to do the absurd thing of living for a future of love and peace that is not yet here.

The disciples of Jesus Christ are the oddest of people; they are those who seek to enter into death in honesty and doubt while shaping their lives toward a future where death is no more, a future that has not yet arrived; for they are people of the cross who hope in the Resurrection. As disciples orientate their lives toward the future, toward the fulfillment of Love, parts of them are put to death. Living for the future means allowing those things in us that are fed by death to be starved; as we seek the future of God in love we must open our being to allow the Spirit of God's Love of Father and Son to destroy all in us that worships death.

We can only do this by finding God in our loss, yearning, and brokenness, for in finding God in death, death is exposed and placed on notice, and now we must abandon it for life. Owen then was right: to love is to have parts of us destroyed, for love lives for the future where death is no more. Love is the power of the future, of the coming of God, calling us to abandon all deception, to put it to death by facing death in the presence of God. (We will pick up this future orientation again in chapter 8.)

STRANGER THAN FICTION

In the movie *Stranger than Fiction* Will Ferrell plays Harold Crick, an uptight insurance adjuster who hides his unhappiness in a rigidly ordered life. As uptight, unlovable Crick falls in love with Ana (Maggie Gyllenhaal), he discovers that his life is actual being written by the novelist Karen Eiffel (Emma Thompson). When he is in the shower or brushing his teeth, he can actually hear her narrating his life. Needing help making sense of this experience, he goes to a local university English professor who enters with him into this journey. Finally, toward the end of the movie Harold confronts the author, Eiffel, who has been convinced that she is writing the best of her many acclaimed novels. Of course freaked out that Harold actually exists and that she has the power to write his destiny, she allows him to read a draft of the novel. Before Harold reads it he takes it to Professor Hilbert, who upon reading it confesses that it is the best book of the author's to date and once released will be a classic, but the whole story rests on Harold dying. There is no other way; the story can't work without it. Harold takes the manuscript and now reads it for himself, concluding that the professor is right: it is beautiful, and he decides that Eiffel should keep the story just as it is.

So the day comes on which Harold is to die. As he walks to his bus stop, as he does every morning, a little boy on a bike falls right in the path of an oncoming bus. Jumping out to save the boy Harold is hit and is apparently dead, just as the novel had stated. But as the next scene dawns we see Harold in a hospital bed, head to toe in casts. The camera pans over him and we hear the professor and Eiffel talk about the changed ending. "It's OK," says Professor Hilbert. "It's not great," returns Eiffel. "It's not bad. *Not* the most amazing piece of American literature in several years, but it's OK," Hilbert asserts. Eiffel is fine with OK. But the professor has another question, "Why," he asks, "did you change the book?" "Lots of reasons," says Eiffel, but mostly, she continues, "because it's a book [originally] about a man who doesn't know he's going to die, but if the man does know that he's going to die and dies anyway . . . dies willingly . . . isn't that the type of man you want to keep alive?"

Jürgen Moltmann says something very similar in his articulation of the cross of Christ and its meaning for the church. He states, "The cross is not and cannot be loved. Yet only the crucified Christ can bring the freedom which changes the world because it is no longer afraid of death."[4] The disciple then is not the one who loves death, but who freely enters death to find its Lord. *And upon entering death discovers the beauty of life.*

Shouldn't Eiffel's words be the words of the world toward the disciple and the church of disciples? They are a people who know they are going to die, who are willing to face death in all its forms, who see death and bear death as their Lord does, and who nevertheless act for life in joy and responsibility. Are these not people who know who they are? Are they not those who have an *identity* that is firm, for it is molded in the heat of honesty, doubt, and absurdity? It is an identity that seeks to enter death to find life. "Christian identity can be understood only as an act of identification with the crucified Christ," Moltmann says, continuing, "Thus the place where the question of identity can meaningfully be asked is the situation of the crisis of identity, brought about by meaningful self-emptying and solidarity."[5] Such people willing to enter the crisis of despair are not finding the death of identity, but a new identity through death.

REFLECTING ON THE STORY OF SCRIPTURE

Saul to Paul

Saul is an Ivy-League-educated guy. He knows his sacred texts, and he knows no Messiah can come from the tree of death; no Messiah can be crucified. It seems in opposition to all he has known, a God of glory found in death, found crucified. He is ready and willing to kill all who would believe this lie, this lie that the glorious and holy God is found in despair and death.

On another excursion to kill those who are worshiping the crucified God Saul is blinded and knocked from his horse. From the light a voice asks, "Saul, Saul, why do you persecute me? I am Jesus" (Acts 9:4-5). From this encounter Saul is transformed to Paul, from the realization that God encounters us not in grandeur but in the despair of God's death Saul becomes Paul who preaches only Christ and him crucified. Paul would travel spreading the message of a God who is known first in the humility of the cross and then in the glory of the temple. When the church of Corinth ridiculed Paul for being less than impressive in stature and speaking ability, Paul owned it and said, "Yes, because this is the way God works. This God of the cross works in paradox, taking what is worthless and making it of value, taking what looks foolish and making it wisdom, taking what looks like death and making it salvation (2 Cor. 4 and 5). The Saul of power is transformed into the Paul of shared suffering and open weakness in the name of Jesus Christ.

DISCUSSION QUESTIONS

- *How does the American church represent this Pauline way of ministry? How are we weak in the strength of Jesus?*

- *How do things change if discipleship is about honesty? How can your local congregation be a place of honesty? What actions could you take?*

- *If doubt is central to discipleship, how do we encourage people to doubt as sign of belief, as faith seeking understanding? How do we do this in membership classes? in Sunday school? in confirmation?*

CHAPTER SEVEN

A FUNERAL FOR THE TRINITY

Community through Death

A
S KARA ANSWERED THE PHONE she couldn't make out what was being said, let alone who was saying it. It was early and she tried to shake the sleep from her mind, hoping it would bring this confusing moment into some kind of coherence. She could only ask from her dazed confusion, "What?" But it was the same frantic noise, repeating the same thing; it was a person whose voice was familiar. "What? What?" she repeated again. Then, as if looking at one of those three-dimensional pictures that suddenly revealed its object from the dots and squares, she realized what was being said. It became clear and horrible, shaking Kara's early-morning being as the frantic stammers became decoded. "My brother! My brother is dead! My brother is dead!!!!" It was Steph, Kara's (my wife's) dear friend, a friend since childhood. Steph's brother Taylor had just hours earlier, at twenty-years-old, been killed in a car accident.

My wife spent the next several days with Steph and her family. Their pain worn deeply on their faces, sorrow as heavy weight on their shoulders. We went to the funeral early. Kara stood with Steph for a while, and throughout the open-casket viewing Steph was strong, comforting Taylor's friends, receiving with grace sorrowful regret. There was strength spilling from her gashed wounds. When the service started, Steph got up to memorialize Taylor. With dignity and poise she spoke of her love for him; with honesty she spoke of Taylor's own yearning and loss. She was broken, it was clear, but she seemed steady and in control; she had forced her broken being to rise to the occasion, to make it through this hour, to be strong.

However, as she talked there were moments when the strength of her determination to make it through showed the depth of the abyss in which she found herself. At points she would say words that relived the deep loss the monster delivers when he arrives. When Steph would say "my brother" it was as if her breath would disappear, her head would tilt and her eyes would reveal a yearning, loss, and brokenness that penetrated every molecule of her person. She could say "Taylor" with strength, able to avoid the hell of the experience by objectifying her brother through a name. There were, after all, millions of Taylors in the world, many of whom she didn't know and who would draw no tears if hearing that some other "Taylor" somewhere had died. But when she said "my brother," Taylor's being could no longer be hidden, for his being was connected to hers. When she said "my brother," Steph was confessing not only that Taylor was gone but also that her brother who had made her a sister had disappeared from existence. With her brother gone, so was part of Steph. They were as they were together—Steph was sister and Taylor was brother. But in her "my brother, oh, my brother" she revealed that his death was such loss that it not only meant his absence, it also meant the loss of her own being. Steph, standing gracefully before family and friends was now in the world differently. She would exist forever from within the crater of her loss, yearning, and brokenness of the disappearance the other, who, at least in part, made her who she was.

DEATH KILLS COMMUNITY WITH THE WEAPON OF SEPARATION

Death destroys community; death is separation, which is what makes it so painful. And it is a separation that seemingly stretches deeper than space. I can live far away from a friend, see him almost never, but when I hear that he has died I find myself stunned. I find myself contemplating that he is gone—*gone*. I have had little contact with him, but now there is no longer even the possibility of encountering him, and he is lost from encountering anyone at all. He has been taken by the monster to a land where community, connection, and encounter is impossible; he has been separated from relating, and there is no being outside of relating, which is what makes death so scary.

I remember being a kid, lying on my bed and thinking about my death, thinking about how one day, at some moment that is coming, I'll pass over, I'll slide from being alive and here to being dead and gone. These thoughts scared the crap out of me. They still do. My whole life is being pulled toward this event in which I will no longer be, that it will be me lying in a casket, looking not quite like myself—it *will be* me.

When I would think about this moment as a kid, I remember thinking that it wouldn't have to be so scary if I didn't have to do it alone, if a friend or even an acquaintance would take the trip from life to death with me. I suppose I was equating the passing from life to death to something like going to junior high, where it felt so much easier to pass from sixth to seventh grade when you were with your friends. In my neighborhood, in those first weeks of junior high all seventh graders walked to school in a horde, about ten of us, meeting every morning, to make the transition survivable. Just like junior high, I imagined it could be easier to pass from life to death if you had someone you knew to live through the transition with. But the impossibility of this very desire is what makes death so terrible.

Death sucks because it separates us from relationship, even relationship with our very bodies. My being is fused with my body. As I type this sentence (to the shame of my high school typing teacher) I am looking at my hands. They are so familiar, they are me; I may in some way be more than them (by the very fact that I can think that I am) but nevertheless they are me. My body is me. I cannot imagine being outside of it (which is why resurrection is such an essential theological point), but more adamantly I cannot imagine someone else being in control of it. I can't contemplate someone else preparing it for a viewing or cutting it open to harvest its parts. It may not matter to me after I die, but it matters to me now; it is me, and I cannot separate myself from my body. But at some point death will extract life from my body, killing me, drowning me forcefully in the shallow water of nothingness, annihilating not only community between me and others, but going to such a vicious extreme as to thrust separation within my very self, within my material body.

THE MUTE BUTTON

Death is relationlessness. That is its ultimate power. Eberhard Jungel explains that this relationlessness is manifest in the fact that death is mute. What he means is that we have our being in relationships of communication. Language reveals that at our core we are made for relationship, but death renders the dead mute; they are lost, they can no longer have communion with us. Like in *Weekend at Bernie's* we may act as if the one dead can still interact and communicate with us, but this must be ultimately judged as pathological or comical (if you're a fan of *Weekend at Bernie's*).

This is why it is a sign of dealing with grief to eventually clean out the room of the one who has died and give things away. When a family or friend refuses to do this, it is clear that they have not allowed themselves to face the fact that this person is gone forever from their communion of communication. When she was alive we knew her around this stuff, we knew her as we interacted with her in this room around this stuff. "Just last week, I thought about how cute

she looked in those jeans, now lying on her floor as if awaiting her, but she will never wear them again." Just last week
she was lying there on her bed, but now she is gone, and
even this stuff—these shirts, shoes, and furniture—once
communicated to us because they were used by our loved
one. But this stuff can no longer communicate, because she
no longer *is*. To hold on to this stuff that can no longer communicate, to keep it just as it was when she was alive, is to
do the absurd thing of trying to make the stuff communicate to us without the being of her person.

We can remember those now gone, even have a day to
memorialize them, but we cannot interact with them. They
have been made forever mute by death. They may (or we
may imagine from our great desire for them to) meet us and
speak to us through a vision, dream, or paranormal experience. But this only witnesses that they are no longer part of
our day-to-day community; if there is some way to communicate beyond the grave, it is an abnormality. And what
makes death so hard is that the one loved, like Steph's
brother, is lost to the normal and regular—to Thanksgiving
dinners, family reunions, and midweek lunchtime drop-
ins. It is around the day-to-day and normal, in communication, that we have something called community.

A FUNERAL FOR THE TRINITY

Death ends and separates all community, and as we saw
in chapter 5, there is no exception for God. As Steph cries
out, "Oh, my brother!" Jesus cries out, "My God, my God,
why have you forsaken me?" The community within the
being of God, the community called Trinity, cannot itself
stand up to the separation of death. Death separates God
from Godself. God allows death to end the very community
of the Trinity itself.

Once there was perfect community between Father, Son,
and Spirit, but now on the cross the Son is lost to death, and
the Father then loses part of his own being as the Son is lost,

just as Steph feels part of herself die, at least the part called "sister," with the death of Taylor. The very self-definition of God, as Father, is annihilated when the Son dies. When the Son is swallowed by nothingness, the very part of the Father that makes the Father a father is obliterated. There are no fathers without sons. Without the relationship of the Father and Son, now that this is gone, the Spirit too is annihilated. For the Spirit is the spirit of the relationship between Father *and* Son, and now there is no longer any *and*, for there is no Son—he has been killed—and there is no Father, for his Son has been overtaken by death. There can be no Father without a Son, and there can be no Spirit without the relationship between Father and Son. The Spirit then tastes the fullness of death as well, for without the relationship the Spirit is not.

The impossible has occurred. The community that has *spoken* creation into being out of non-being has been rendered mute by itself being pushed into nothingness. The Trinity as the community that stands over and against nothingness, speaking life and possibility out of its darkness, now takes darkness within itself, allowing it to destroy fully its community. The cross is the death of the community of God in Godself. The God who had originally spoken being out nonbeing, by asserting that non-being was not good, has now taken the *not good* of nonbeing into God's very being.[1]

THE TRINITY IS PUT BACK TOGETHER

But, now that God in Godself has died, now that the God who speaks being out of non-being has been pinned and the community of God has been annihilated by death, now that death has done the audacious act of separating the community of Godself, we see that God's Love, the Love of the relationship between Father and Son, is stronger than death. We see that out of the heaviness of death God brings life; from cross comes resurrection. The community of God, the Trinity itself, is put back together around death, loss, yearning, and brokenness. The Love of God is perfected for it is a Love strong enough to bring new life out of death. The three that are one have experienced the fullness of death; death has now become part of their community. Where death, loss, and brokenness had rendered the communication of the Trinity's communion mute, it is now suffering and new life out of death that is to be proclaimed—to the ends of the earth. Where once death silenced, now the death of God gives voice. Death itself has been overcome in the community of Trinity by the Trinity entering death through the cross. Death can no longer be determinative—not for Benjamin, not for Denny, not for Taylor, not for any experiencing loss—because death has been taken into the Trinity itself. Benjamin, Denny, and Taylor now exist through their own death in relationship (in community) with God's very self. Those overwhelmed by medical bills, lost jobs, and failed loves are taken into the community of God. For death has been placed within and between Godself, and now all who die are found in communion with the one (as Father, Son, and Spirit) who knows the fullness of death. God overcomes death's power to separate and destroy community by dying and therefore making community with all those who experience death.

This means suffering now rests eternally at the heart of God's community with Godself. Shared suffering and despair for the sake of Love is the very fabric of God's own community. Thus the very community of the Trinity is opened up to us, to humanity, for we, like God, know suffering, despair, and death, and it is now through these universal realities that we find communion with God. It is through these realities that God speaks to us as the one who shares in our despair. The necessary criteria to be in community with God, after the cross, is suffering, because God knows loss, yearning, and brokenness. Any human being who has known in any way the same is welcomed into communion with God. And it is through this communion with God through our deaths that we are given new community where at the center is God's own Love as Father and Son through death. God takes death into God's own self so that the community of Trinity itself might be opened up to humanity. Our destiny is death. There is no stopping the monster, but now the monster is tethered between the Love of the Father and Son; now our despair cannot separate and isolate us, but instead, in a wonderful paradox, places us in communion with God.

Therefore, to have community with God is to have community through suffering and despair that rests at the heart of the Trinity's own community, through the cross. And it is only through our own suffering and despair, our own wrestling with death, that we are taken into the death, suffering, and despair of God that exists in the life of the Love of Father and Son through the Spirit. Because God has entered fully into nonbeing, it is through nonbeing that we have community with God. This is why Luther wants so badly for us to face death and despair. For after the cross and resurrection, after the division of death in the Trinity is healed, it is through death that we find community with God and one another, for death is placed between the Father and Son. The very community that makes God, God, the Trinity itself, is constructed around the Love that knows death, the Love that places death between the Love of Father and Son, so now all that suffer are placed into community with God.

A TRINITARIAN THEOLOGY FOR THE CHURCH

The recovery of Trinitarian theology (especially a social Trinity) for missional and ecclesiological purposes has tended to see the Trinity as a model or analogy for how the church should be. Because the Trinity is a community of persons without hierarchy, the church should be a place where people are important, relationships are central, and hierarchy is not practiced. While this may be helpful to a point, it ignores the difference in kind between the community of the Trinity and the community of human sinful beings, even one called "church." It is not these personal or antihierarchical themes that the Trinity opens up to the church (not directly at least). Rather, as the community that overcomes death by placing death at the center of its life, the Trinity calls the church to be a suffering community that makes loss, yearning, and brokenness the center of its existence.

It is suffering, as God's act, that is central to the church. The church cannot control God's act; the community of the Trinity may be perfect in its unity and differentiation, but the church never can be. But this is not its call; its call is not to control God's action in its own operations, but to be open to experience an encounter with God through its humanity. And it is through suffering and despair that God meets us, that God takes us up into the Love of the Trinity; it is here that Steph's cry, "Oh, my brother," is joined in the suffering of God.

The church is not a community that is trying to emulate the Trinity (the life of the Trinity is hidden to us); the church is the community that is to place loss, yearning, and brokenness at its center, for through the cross loss, yearning, and brokenness are now at the center of the Trinity. The church is to dialogue about failure and pain, trusting that in so doing the church as weak and suffering community is taken up into the life of God in Godself. The church is a broken, suffering, weak community that witnesses in its willingness to face these realities that God in Godself has borne death, meeting us all (those in the church and not) in the midst of our loss, yearnings, and brokenness. It seems that this is what Paul is after both in his own life and in his leadership of the church (2 Cor. 12:9; 1 Cor. 1:20-30). Paul seeks a church that embraces its weakness, for the church is the community that serves the world by worshiping the God who has placed death between the Love of Father and Son. The church is the community that serves the world and therefore encounters God by facing death, confronting it in its horror, by refusing to allow it to render mute those found in loss, yearning, and brokenness. The church, for Paul, is the people of the crucified Christ, the community of the cross.

The church is not a powerful community, but a weak community that, as such, doesn't fear allowing suffering people to speak. In a world that has no place to allow suffering and death to be spoken of, the church, in its following of a crucified God, makes its life around the articulation of its members' and its neighbors' brokenness. The church is the community that speaks to the world of death. It is the community that calls a thing what it is. It is like the church I know on the West Coast that uses film, deep human dramas, to lead them into conversation, but the kind of conversation that sends them not only into deep personal reflection but also out into their neighborhood to care for the broken and homeless. The church speaks of death and yet also articulates the promise that death itself has been taken into the life of God. The church has tried to make its life around program offerings, cultural relevance, and dynamic personalities, but it is the call to witness to a suffering God by speaking of suffering and death that makes the church the community of the crucified.[2]

WHERE THE WEAK ARE WELCOME

The great power of death is its ability to separate. To separate four-year-olds from their friends, to separate fifth-graders from their fathers, to separate sisters from their brothers—the power of the monster of death is to cut us off, to make us alone. But when we are together as the church, speaking of death and allowing others to speak of their brokenness, then suffering is no longer the dark trail to being alone and separated, but is instead transformed into the horrible sacrament of our shared life. It is horrible, because it is death and suffering—it sucks. But it is a sacrament because within its horrible ordinariness, God, because of the cross, has promised to encounter us. We grieve and wish for our suffering to be no more, but as we speak of it we are drawn closer and closer together, for we are not only communing with one another, but with the very God of the cross.

The church, then, should be the oddest of communities in our world, the oddest group of people. A community of people whose life is constructed around sharing in each other's suffering for the purposes of encountering the God of the cross. It should be a community unlike all other communities, one that treasures it weakest members, offers children, the disabled, and the sick not only seats of honor but places of leadership. Like the very small Congregational church in Arcadia, California, where one volunteer liturgist was blind and read scripture from a Braille Bible and every week Mary, a mentally disabled woman, led them in prayer—prayers that rambled in coherence but were nevertheless the lifeblood of the church's communion with one another and God.

This congregation revealed that the church is a weak community, *not* in the fact that it is pathetic, but in its willingness to face nothingness and death in search for possibility and life. The church believes the weak hold a perspective of reality that the so-called strong cannot know, a perspective of a God who chooses death and weakness (a cross) over glory.

The church's distinction in the world is not its morality or even its joy (especially if we define joy close to happiness). The church in the world is like all others: the members of the church know loss, yearning, and brokenness, but its distinction is that this community, unlike most other communities, refuses to ignore or deny these realities, but rather in the Love of God seeks to enter them, seeking and finding God alongside and within our brokenness—this is sure joy!

FROM THE DEATH OF COMMUNITY TO NEW COMMUNITY THROUGH DEATH

In chapter 3, I argued that community has all but died in our world. I argued that communities have to be built on some kind of obligation, that they have to be built on more than choice, preference, or taste. In our consumerist world obligation is a bad word, making community very difficult, making it always close to death. When life changes, when your tastes change, your community dies.

The church has often tried two strategies as it has tacitly confronted this obligation-allergic society. It has either held to its traditional stance (wishing for a time when people felt obligated to go to church), seeking to make people feel guilty for not feeling obligated to the church. Or, knowing that strategy is quite flawed, the church has sought to exist within the world of our hyperchoice, making itself consumable. Yet, ironically while more people may choose to come to church, the more successful these churches are the more they are void of community. If obligation is dead, but, as social theorists tell us, obligation (or something like it) is necessary for community, then what options does the church have? If community is dead and yet the church is a community, as we have asserted in this chapter, then what is this community constructed on?

Just as the community of Trinity is not constructed around obligation but is bound one to another through the Love that knows loss, yearning, and brokenness, therefore the church is to be a community in a world where community has died. The church, to be a community, must build its life around practices and actions of shared suffering. The glue that can hold a community together, especially in a world where community has died, is mutual sharing in each other's loss, yearning, and brokenness.

It is like the moment that happened at our church just last week. In the middle of the pastor taking prayer requests, requests that seemed benign and regular, Kathryn raised her hand and said, "This Tuesday I go in for my tests," pausing as fear spread across her face, she continued, "I don't know what will happen; I don't know what is wrong with me and I'm so scared." In her confession our hearts were drawn together and we prayed, not as a religious act but as a plea for the God of suffering Love to encounter *us* in Kathryn's fear and in our love for her. Now, through Kathryn's confession of suffering, together, sharing in each other's lives, we were together before the God of the cross. It is in these moments that we are the church, that we have community, for it is in these moments in our weakness and facing death that we are witnessing to the God of the cross who gives us community through death.

REFLECTING ON THE STORY OF SCRIPTURE

The Father and the Prodigal Son

The parable of the prodigal son is a story from the lips of Jesus that is filled with despair. A father with two sons, the younger of the whom wishes the father dead, takes his money, and leaves him. Off in a faraway country he wastes his money on prostitutes and gambling, and soon finds himself broken, lost, up against the death of what was, the death of his dreams. His father is at home in despair, hoping for his son's return, but every day there is no sign, no message. He could be dead for all he knows, dead and gone, with only their final argument to close the chapter on their relationship.

In despair the son returns home, ashamed, ready to be a slave to his father. He knows he has hurt his father deeply, and hurt often causes us to look for retribution more than forgiveness. But seeing the son on the horizon the father runs to him. In actions unbecoming of a man of his standing, he races to his boy, embracing him and again calling him *son*. He has received him back from death; he was gone, but has now been resurrected. Through the despair of his broken heart, a heart that chose to face his hurt rather than hide from it in anger or rigidity, he has been given back his promise; he has been given his son.

And such is the kingdom of God, Jesus tells his listeners. His Father is one who enters the despair of loss, yearning, and brokenness so that God might welcome all back to be loved in the Love of the Father to Son. This God, Jesus reveals, is a God who will suffer yearning and insult and abandonment and the pain of children's shame for the sake of love.

DISCUSSION QUESTIONS

- *Upon reflection on this parable what strikes you? What seems most surprising?*

- *What does it mean if the Trinity has gone through death? How does that change the way we think about ministry?*

- *If, as sociologists assert, communities must be built around obligation, but obligation is missing in our context, how do you imagine the sharing of our suffering as a way of binding us together? How could this be done in the worship service itself?*

CHAPTER EIGHT

DOES DEATH WEAR A HELMET?

Justice through Death

HE WAS QUIETLY DUNKING a cookie, the remains of some astronaut, knight, or *Star Wars* storm trooper costume still hanging from his skinny limbs. It was a perfect spring afternoon. As he dunked, up to his knuckles in milk, the sun poked through the big oak tree in our front yard, spilling its rays through our front window and splashing the dining room table Owen sat at with light. Owen dunked in pleasure and contemplation. A long morning of running and playing does that. The silence was beautiful, the pause in the day perfect. But with his last bite Owen broke the quiet calm with another question. He had spent all morning moving from one costumed character to another, from light sabers to football helmets to space ships made with the stained cushions of our couch. Owen never looked at us, communicating that his inquiry was borne deep in his being, a question he had been wrestling with, at least since he made his first dunk. Sitting in a chair too big for him, Owen asked, "Does death wear a helmet?"

"Does death wear a helmet?" At first his question seemed too odd to answer. I feared his ginger snap had been laced with some hallucinogenic drug. But as I stammered and contemplated what to respond, I realized only silence was appropriate, not because the question was so illogically absurd, but because it was so deeply profound. Draped in his costume, battles with evil droids, pirates, and enemy football players still dripping from his imagination, Owen sought to place his imaginary reality into what was real. All bad guys wear helmets it seemed to him, especially scary bad guys like Darth Vader. If his fictional bad guys always seemed to have a helmet on, then what about the monster of death? Does death wear a helmet?

I think it is true. I think death does wear a helmet. We too often think of death as only the end, as only the last moment, but death puts on its hard hat and goes to work much earlier than the last moments before we stop breathing. Death is at work in the lonely longing of friendless fourth-graders, in the failure of a husband and wife to communicate, in the depression and defeat of another failure to figure out what it is we are to do with our lives. Death wears a helmet, not only because death collides with us before our last breath, knocking us around from our beginning to our end, but also because death has constructed places for itself within the very structures in which we live. Death is experienced not just in our individual feelings, not just in the action we do or neglect to do to each other, but in the very institutions and bureaucracies that organize our lives. Death wears a helmet because death is found in the structures of society.

DEATH IN THE OFFICIAL UNIFORM OF OUR SOCIETAL STRUCTURES

This is what makes death so ultimately scary. The monster knocks you down when the letter from the insurance company reveals your sick daughter has no coverage, when the school system in your neighborhood cannot educate your children, and the police cannot be trusted, or when you are paid less and overlooked for promotion because of your gender or ethnicity. Death wears a helmet not only because such experiences feel like being tackled by a 350-pound linebacker, but also, and maybe more directly, because it appears that such things are just the way it is. Death wears the logo of institutions and structures of our society on its helmet, indicating that it is only doing its job, hiding that it is the fullness of death, that it is the reaper.

True despair is confrontation with realities like racism and poverty—realities that seem to exist in the very foundations of our society; realities that no one individually wills to exist, but nevertheless, because they have burrowed themselves within the very structure of our lives (structures like the economy, political establishment, the educational system, etc.) confront us beyond our individual will. They have become cancers that feed other organisms with blood, allowing them to grow strong and powerful at the expense of other parts of the body. Yet, though we will for them not to be, death whispers, through the face mask of its institutional helmet, that these realities are necessary.

We are told that to extract them is to threaten society, the whole body, with death. Therefore, it is better to allow the cancers of racism and poverty to continue than to threaten our way of life. We will watch them carefully, the monster promises, but we cannot risk extracting them. Markets would collapse, societal order lost if we removed them. "And you fear that, don't you?" the monster asks. And many of us, especially those of us who attend church, nod our heads, write a charitable check, and move on, allowing the cancer to continue, trying to deny that many are withering while others are feasting because of the cancer in our structures.

It is the monster of death who says these thing to us, the monster that wants only separation and destruction, but he is wearing a helmet with official institutional logos on it. He seems so honorable, so in control. Like a company man, he has distinguished himself within the structure of our society; he has covered up the blood of Benjamin and Denny that drips from his lips, behind his institutional helmet. He speaks of order and greater good, but he wants only death.

Wearing his helmet he convinces me of two things. First, he convinces me that it is in my own interest to toe the line and not question the death in the structures, or as liberal

Christianity often does, to discuss issues *ad nauseam* in an intellectual manner until they mean nothing. Like fencing off protest zones at political conventions, the monster of death is willing to allow liberal intellectual Christians to write about and discuss such issues, knowing it means little to regular people who suffer under his official licentious tyranny. Liberal Christianity's assertions are fenced off behind their intellectual diatribes, unable to connect with real people and therefore have little impact, so the monster allows them to make their arguments, blowing off steam, allowing the structures themselves to remain as they are—bent toward death.[1]

I'm convinced so easily by the monster that if I question his rule in the structures too forcefully I'll put my house or my child's college tuition at stake, that my own educational achievement will be devalued. He is wearing a helmet, but he is a gangster, intimidating me to toe the line or else feel it where it hurts. So I find myself contemplating how, with just another two thousand dollars here I could fix my roof, another two thousand there and I could jump start Maisy's college tuition. Soon I can contemplate five other areas that need two thousand dollars, and now I'm convinced I need more money. I'm anxious and threatened by anyone or anything that might keep me from my imaginary need for another two grand. And the monster, behind his perfectly shined helmet, just smiles while my anxiety of pretend need keeps me existentially committed to the structures as the way they are.

Second, standing there in his shiny helmet, he convinces me that there is little, after all, that I can do. Issues like racism and poverty are huge. What can I do? I'm sick they exist, but they are burrowed into the structures, and I have little power to change the structures—and I wouldn't want to anyway, he reminds me. Standing in his helmet the monster of death deceivingly asserts that he is for the greater good, that he is wearing his helmet so right is rewarded and wrong is punished. Don't mind that our prisons are disproportionately filled with young black males who have little economic options in their neighborhood other than the underground economy, for they did bad, and now must be punished. *The helmet-wearing monster asks us to focus on behavior and not examine conditions.*

THE CROSS IS ABOUT
CONDITIONS OVER BEHAVIOR

But this is where we are pushed back to the cross, for the cross is the battle with nothingness. The cross is about God taking on nothingness to overcome nothingness, so it is about conditions and not simply behavior. The cross is the bearing of the reality of death. This is its salvation: it overcomes the conditions of death with life; it cages the monster within Godself. The cross is not about behavior, or simply about God paying for the bad things we do so we can be good boys and girls again. The cross is about overcoming the monster; it is about confronting with God's own being the conditions of being human, of facing death. It is about confronting loss, yearning, and brokenness within ourselves but also within our structures, for our structures impinge on us as conditions.

No one wants there to be poverty, but the conditions of our structures allow for poverty to nevertheless exist. The cross, then, for it to mean anything, must have more to do with our reality than simply solving our problems of bad behavior; it must have something to do with our conditions. Ultimately, as I have argued throughout Part One, we must see our condition of death not only as an individual situation but also as a societal reality as well; death is within our structures.

The cross, confronting our conditions and not simply our behavior, does not eliminate the judgment of God. We are in need of being judged by God not only for our behavior but more primarily for our conditions. The inner-city youth must come under judgment for selling drugs, but so too must the conditions he exists in that push him to this behavior. His behavior must be taken into the life of God, judged as serving death, but he can only be free if the cross also takes the conditions he exists in into Godself as well, judging them as the works of death. Therefore, God judges by loving. God condemns the conditions of death by taking them into Godself, calling us to live in and for the Love of God and therefore to deny those actions (behaviors) that serve the conditions of death.

From the location of the cross we can see that under that shiny helmet it is death in our structures and it is death's work as a condition that is the issue. But God is the God of life, the God who speaks life into being out of the nothingness of death. God is the God who will always be found on the side of life, for this God has gone so far as to be seen as weak to bring life out of death. God calls his people to serve God by standing for life against death. But the cross reveals that this standing for life can only be done by taking on death. The cross as the taking on of death within God's very self is not about morality. It is about life and death, nothingness and possibility, or to say it more correctly, it is about life out of death.

THE CHURCH BEYOND RIGHT AND WRONG

The church so often wants to do what is right, but when this is our goal we quickly are moved away from conditions to behavior. We want to do things to help the poor, but we are not willing to bear their conditions, to see that their conditions are tangled within the multiple structures in our society. When faith is simply about right and wrong, then it is so easy to allow the death in our structures to remain unconfronted. We fear getting too close to those experiencing injustice, for fear that their behavior will contaminate us, or in self-righteousness we hate those who are too individualistic to see the political and religious rightness of our position. Both liberals and conservatives focus on good versus bad (on behavior), but the cross ultimately calls us to see life and death. It often seems liberals want to *do* good and conservatives want to *be* good, but neither want to enter death for the sake of life, neither want to make their very lives in the despair of existence.

The church is not the community in the world that is good or even moral; the church is the people in the world who face death, who enter death for the sake of life. Like a church I know on the East Coast that refuses to do mission trips, trips they feel too easily place their people in a stance of doing, making the people they serve into a commodity, allowing them to do good and then forget. This church has decided to invite their people to simply be with others in need, to share in their conditions, to share with them their own condition, trusting that in the mutual sharing of conditions they are sharing in a life of action in the presence of God.

The church speaks for the voiceless (the poor, the oppressed, the sick) not because it is the right thing to do, but because these people are experiencing death, because death insistently confronts them in the very unjust structures in society. Therefore, the church must engage—not because the church is a political community, but because it is a people who can be found anywhere there is death; for it is our vocation to enter death and bear it, for God is found in our condition between nothingness and possibility, between life and death. The church participates in the life of God by participating in these realities; by speaking of death in the structures, it speaks for life in the despair of injustice.[2]

This means Christianity is *not* about morality, doing right, or being good. From the perspective of the cross this cannot be Christianity's primary concern, because God in the cross has placed the condition of death incubated in our societal structure within the history and life of Godself. Therefore, Christianity is about facing death in its fullness for the sake of encountering the God of life. But we can only encounter this God if we are willing to face death—and that includes the insidious death sponsored by our helmet-wearing monster, the death that festers in the structures of our society.

A GOD WHO BEARS INJUSTICE

God takes death into God's very self for the sake of life. Now, as we said in the last chapters, death exists between the Love of the Father to Son. Brokenness and impossibility are borne in the division of God's very self in the death of the Son, the loss of the Father, and annihilation of the Spirit. Now, the very impossibility of our structures, their very injustice as the reality of death, is taken into the being of God. God is found in the despair of dirty apartments, drug corners, and out-of-control classrooms. The cross reveals that God battles injustice by bearing injustice (this is what Martin Luther King Jr. sought in his nonviolent resistance). God stands against injustice by making injustice the very conditions that God exists in. God takes the death of injustice into God's very self; now the voracious conditions of all of death, even the death of injustice, existence in the inner life of God. God has been crucified; God has had the very structures of God's creation turn on God.

This means that those experiencing the despair of injustice are found caught up in God's very self. God is found with those in the condition of injustice. In the despair of injustice God is concretely found bearing the very conditions of injustice for the sake of life and new possibility. God takes injustice into Godself, placing it between the Love of the Father and Son. Now, placed between the Love of the Father and Son, injustice is broken; the very structures that separated the Father from the Son are overcome with life.[3]

We confess, because of the cross, that those suffering despair under the injustice of the structures of society are placed in relationship with God. Their experience of injustice has bound them to the very being of God, for injustice itself has been taken into Godself. The church must then go to the broken to have Christ at all, to even those broken by the very injustice of the structures that benefit so many of us. Yet, the church often refuses to go, sending a check instead, because the homeless and addicted seem to threaten us. We condemn their broken humanity as due to poor choices and bad behavior; therefore, we will send resources and missionaries to take Jesus to them. But the homeless and addicted do not primarily need what the church can bring them (though they may); rather, the church needs what the homeless and addicted bring it. They bring the brokenness of their humanity, crushed by the structures of society, as the very sacrament of God's presence. For the church to be with them is itself to be caught up in God's very self. To be the people of the cross is to be the people crushed by the structures of the helmet-wearing monster.

As Paul has reminded us we are already dead in Christ, therefore we live in his Love, so we can be brave enough to call a thing what it is, to point out the death in our structures, even if it threatens another two grand for me and therefore feels like risk.[4]

The death of injustice exists within Godself for the sake of breaking it. In the resurrected body of Christ we are promised that all death, even the death of injustice, is passing away, that a new reality is on its way, that God has acted by taking on death, therefore destroying its determinative power, and has inaugurated a future that has its source in the Love of the Father and Son that conquers death. This inaugurated future will sooner or later be all that there is. The kingdom of suffering Love, the kingdom that is built from within death is coming, and it is a kingdom, Jesus tells us, that will be inherited by the poor. It will be a kingdom where those experiencing the death of unjust structures are given new life. It will be a future where death has no say, where love reigns as wholeness and freedom.

LIVING FOR A FUTURE NOT YET HERE

The church is called to exist in death as it exists for God's future. It exists in death because it knows from the view of the cross that this coming of God's future only happens through death. *But death is not the church's obsession; no, the church's obsession is God and God's future,* a future where death is no more, where death that has been insidiously grafted within our structures is destroyed, where the hungry are fed, the oppressed find freedom, and the sick are healed. The church exists in death, for if it doesn't it has no footing in reality; but standing in death the church lives and acts for the future.

The helmet-wearing monster's lie that in the end there is little we can do is seen as a false assertion. Like all good liars his statement has enough truth in it that we often decide he must be right—the issues of injustice are tangled and overwhelming, and we are always unsure whether solving one problem will not lead to more. Overcoming the oppression of one group will make another group oppressed. The church has no power to wipe away the injustice in the world; the poor will always be with us, Jesus stated. But the church is to take on a completely different perspective; the church is to be the community that lives in death by giving its attention and action toward God's future. The church feeds the poor, gives shelter to the homeless and help to the ill, not because it naively imagines that it can in so doing make hunger, homelessness, and sickness disappear. When the church acts in such a way, when it vigorously gives voice, feeds, shelters, and cares for those thrust into death by the structures, it is living for the future of God that has not yet come, but is coming. Like the church in Canada that, now that its beautiful cathedral has only twenty people in it, has opened its doors to the homeless and outcasts, reforming its life around them not to solve their problems but to be the community that joins in their lives, placing high-powered executives at the same Communion table as HIV-infected drug users.

The church is the absurd community that lives for a future that is not here—a future where there is no injustice. Jesus calls his disciples to be these absurd people who live in a way where the first are last and the last are first, but not because this is the way the world is and therefore it will make us successful and happy—the world is quite the opposite of this. But the church is called to this backwardness of life because the backwardness of the cross reveals that this is the way of God's future, and we are called now to be the people that bend our lives toward a future that has not yet arrived.

Therefore, the church acts now to overcome injustice not because it believes it can solve all problems of death in the world but because in facing the death of injustice it witnesses concretely in its life that the day is coming, and in small ways is already here in the church's own life, where the death in the structures of society will gave way to a new world, a world where death has been completely consumed in the Love of the Father and Son through the Spirit. It is a lie to say there is nothing we can do so we should do nothing, for even in the church's small pathetic action God's future is witnessed to, the Kingdom comes in mustard seeds and old ladies who sweep their house looking for lost coins. The Kingdom is coming when the church faces death and acts for God's future; the church lives for God's future when it acts for justice within the structures of death. But there can be no justice without facing death; there can be no justice of God that is not borne by entering death and living and acting for God's future.

THE NEW AUTHORITY OF GOD'S FUTURE

As we saw in chapter 2, authority has died in our culture; doubt has replaced it. But this is only bad news to the church if is about right and wrong, if it is about itself solving all the problems in the world, if it is about aligning itself with a past tradition. But as we have seen, this is not the church's mission. The church stands on a new authority, a new authority that is found in death, an authority that is not about rightness but about faithfulness, that is not about behavior but about conditions. The new authority that is born in death is the authority of God's future. We are called to make our authority the condition of God's coming future. The Bible is our trusted and faithful witness that pushes us to be the people of God for God's future. Our authority is found in death, for it is in death that we encounter the God of the future calling us to mold our lives after God's Kingdom as the new way of being in the world. Where modenity places us in the present and pushes into a future born from the present, the disciple of a crucified God stands in the present, calling a thing what it is, awaiting God's act that comes out of the future, not tethered to the present, but born from a new eschatological reality.

REFLECTING ON THE STORY OF SCRIPTURE

Abraham

Abraham has been given his son from the dead. Isaac stands as the fulfillment of the promise. There is Isaac playing before the fire, a witness that from the despair of elderly Sarah comes the promise. God waited until it was all but impossible, until her cry for a baby had settled deep inside her with the force to break her heart. But from her broken heart God has acted, God has given her a child, and the promise to Abraham is revived.

But now Abraham receives word that the little boy of the promise, the one born from the despair, is to be taken up the mountain, is to be given to death. The despair of Abraham must be heavier than ever before, confusion must utterly disorientate him. Here he is, here is Isaac, here lives the promise, and now he must die—and die by the hand of the one who has yearned for him for so long.

Abraham takes him up the mountain, sharpens his knife, and prepares to do what he wishes not to: he sharpens his knife in despair so that he might kill the promise. He ties the boy down and raises his knife, and with all the force he can muster he swings, in rage and despair he swings his knife to end the boy quickly. But in his swing of despair God acts. God comes near and the angel stops Abraham, resurrecting Isaac and for a second time giving him to his father through the door of despair. Holding the boy and muttering apologies, Abraham is given again the promise out of despair: out of brokenness comes fulfillment, out of death comes life. Just as Isaac had entered the world from death, he is given back to his father from death. Abraham, and his coming nation, can never forget that its origins rest in the promise of God, the promise that comes through death.

DISCUSSION QUESTIONS

- *What are your reactions to Abraham's situation? Abraham's response? Why would God ask him to do this?*

- *Are there things in your life that God has asked you to take up the mountain and put to death?*

- *This chapter argues that death is in the structures of our society, that death often deceives us into holding tightly to things for fear that we are vulnerable without them. Do you see this in our society? Do you see this in your context? in your congregation?*

- *The chapter also argues that conditions are more important to give attention to than simply behavior. What actions or practices might you take to draw people into reflecting on conditions?*

CHAPTER NINE

CHRISTIAN FAITH IS A SECRET THAT MUST BE KEPT

Hope through Death

IT WAS EARLY SPRING. Only piles of dirty snow remained, plowed in midwinter into huge mounds to clear parking lots and driveways, now slowly melting like glaciers. These dirty snow mounds stood as monuments to the long winter we had survived. Winter had broken and the warmth and energy of a new season was upon us. It was only fifty degrees, but after a winter mostly near or below zero, a day of near fifty degrees brings out shorts, Frisbees, and filled sidewalks in the upper Midwest. I would imagine it an absurd sight to a Californian or Floridian to see pale, pasty people excitedly walking in shorts and tank tops, reveling in forty-five degrees. And even for us, a forty-five-degree day in September comes with complaints and the layering of sweatshirts. But after the cold winter forty-five or fifty degrees is the mercy that promises that summer is on its way, that the cold is behind us, making forty-five or fifty feel like eighty, therefore deserving absurd celebration.

It was in the middle of this seasonal transition that Kara's (my wife's) grandfather died. It was not unexpected; he was in his mid-eighties and suffering from dementia and other ailments. Already removed from his own house, he was spending what seemed inevitably his final months with his daughters and grandchildren. The early spring phone call that brought the news came expectedly, but with sadness. Kara knew that he was fading, but word now that he was gone nevertheless forced her breath from her, sending her chest to chase it with quick inhales. "Granddad is gone," she said as she hung up the phone. Collecting herself she loaded Owen into the car and left for church.

Halfway to church her rational side, which knew that this was inevitable, dissolved, and on the 94 freeway she started to sob. Wiping her tears she looked in the rearview mirror, tipping it to see Owen, who was pinned to his car seat by the straps that gripped his freshly retrieved spring coat that came from our basement. "I'm crying because I am sad, Owen," Kara said.

"Why?" asked Owen, a question that so easily slips from his lips that he often asks it to his own answers. Kara continued, attentively, recognizing this "why" was not just the constant activity of his little mind, but had it origins in the presence of her tears. "I'm sad," she said forthrightly, "because my grandpa is dead. Granddad is gone and that makes me sad." Owen sat quietly for a few seconds, attentively looking out the window as Kara took deep breaths and wiped away her tears.

As they exited the freeway, Owen broke the silence, his face lighting up, "But mommy!" Owen said, lowering his voice and leaning forward with a dramatic stage whisper. "I have a secret! In the end Jesus is coming back and death will die and Granddad will be alive again!" He leaned back in great satisfaction, and with eyes wide open, he concluded by nodding and reiterating, "Mommy, it's a secret!"

And it is a secret! It is not the kind of secret that is kept because you want to keep to yourself whatever information you possess. It isn't a secret because we are shameful of what such knowledge might mean. It is a secret because it is the most beautiful, wonderful thing that could be imagined. Death dying, death being no more, never again able to separate; all those lost will be found. Benjamin and me again climbing an apple tree, Denny walking Jared back to their family car, arms around each other in the dusk of a finished game, the lonely bound in friendship, those unable to communicate found in laughter and connections. It is a secret because every cell in our bodies yearns for it to be so. It is a secret because it is so wonderful and beautiful that the earth shakes with anticipation that it might be true. It is a secret because everything else in our lives points in the other direction. It is a secret because it is the most wonderful of hopes that though our creaturely destiny is death, this destiny has been split through, revealing a new reality where life comes out of death.

THE ELMO FACTOR: THE DIFFERENCE BETWEEN HOPE AND OPTIMISM

And this, after all, is hope. We tend to think that hope is optimism, that to be a hopeful person is to be a person who is always looking on the bright side, who is positive. And I'm not saying it is bad to be positive; positive people tend to have a lot of friends, tend to be easy to be around. I'm always shocked watching *Sesame Street* at how positive Elmo is and how his positive disposition is so attractive. Elmo is one optimistic little dude! But I wouldn't call Elmo hopeful. The mother walking the hall of the children's hospital anticipating the day when she can bring her son home again, washing his body as his strength is depleted, is hopeful. She is the one who acts for the future—a future that seems so far away. She is hopeful because though she is in darkness, she yearns (even a yearning that includes her action) for the slightest of light of a promised future. Elmo is just happy in the moment; Elmo knows no death that makes real hope possible.

Hope is different from optimism in its very orientation to time. Optimism clothes itself in the present, seeking to make the present good through positive thinking. Optimism says this terrible job isn't that bad; I'm confident that if I stay upbeat my dream job will be right around the corner. Optimism, then, is cemented in the present, seeking positivity to make tomorrow's present better (more enjoyable and happier) than today.

141

We all need some optimism. Optimism isn't bad, but optimism cannot confront the monster of death. Optimism can only hide from the monster, ignoring its force. Optimism when pushed to its extreme tries the delusional act of dressing up the monster in a polka-dot dress, seeking to force death to play tea with us. Optimism must seek to deny death because death stands like a fortress between our optimistic todays and our better tomorrows. You can be as optimistic as you want (and it may have health benefits and make you more friends), but no matter how optimistic you are standing in the present you cannot avoid the fact that death will have its way with you. On some tomorrow a car will cross over the median, your son will have learning problems, your health will fail you, your obsession with positivity, to optimistically deny that your present is only unfolding to death, will eventually catch up with you.

But hope stands in an altogether different orientation to time. Hope is born in the future—a future that is not out ahead us, but that is a completely new reality, even now in small ways breaking into our lives. Hope is trust that though the monster may take me, though death may strike me, it cannot destroy me, for a future is on its way that stands in direct opposition to my present. A future is on its way that has no place for death, where death has been extracted and destroyed, where death has been evaporated by the white hot heat of God's Love. This future (in its finality) is not here yet, but hope knows that it is on its way.

Hope says, "This job sucks, but there is a future where disappointment and impossibility give way to the fullness of life." Hope says, "I will anticipate even now, even in this time, such a future, but I will trust that even if I am stuck here for what feels like forever I will remember and mold my life after the future I trust in."

Hope is qualitatively different from optimism, because hope bears death; hope seeks a future not by ignoring or denying death (looking on the bright side) but by living through it. Hope seeks to live honestly in the now by giving its attention to the future, seeking for the future even now to break into our lives. Hope is that mother who washes her son, lifting his body into her arms, embracing his frailty, pushing his body to hers. She washes him because she loves him, because her love for him pushes deep into the darkness of his condition, not as a final fatalistic destination, but as a way of embracing what is so that she might be with him and hope for the day when he can again wash his own body, when he takes her by his strong arms into his chest as life spills from his pores.

THE CHURCH IS <u>NOT</u> IN THE OPTIMISM BUSINESS, BUT LIVES FROM THE SECRET

She confronts the threat of his death not in optimism, but in hope. Optimism says, "Something good will come out of this experience." Hope says, "In the midst of this hell God will act." In the midst of this present hell of death God's future will bring the fullness of life. Optimism is positivity; hope is trust. The church is not in the business of optimism; that is not its function (though the powerful in society may want it to be so). Optimism is for Hallmark, not for a community that worships a crucified God. When optimism is the church's business then we allow it to screen us from seeing reality. The church is not in the business of optimism and positivity but of trust in a new reality that will be born within this broken one.

And it is a secret because it is an altogether different reality that we hope for. Optimism needs no secret, because it is looking for the silver lining in the present of this reality. Optimism speaks incessantly, fearing that if it stops framing this reality in a positive manner it will be annihilated by the nothingness all around us. But hope is a secret that calls for silence, contemplation, and deep reflection. Hope bubbles up from deep within our being that is so close to nothingness, making its way to our lips in fear and trembling. We find ourselves choking on the wonder of its possibility; we find that contemplating it forces us to speak lower; because we are hoping in an altogether different reality, in the dawn of God's future, where death is not optimistically given face paints and cotton candy to hold, but is obliterated in the fullness of life in God's Love. Hope is a secret because it is trust in a wholly new reality, not just this reality shined with the spit of optimistic positivity.

The cross is the overcoming of God with death; death has itself destroyed the Trinity. But the Trinity is the source of life, and death has done the audacious, it has sought to overcome life itself, to overcome with nonbeing the One who speaks being out of nothing for the sake of Love. So from this broken reality, from the death of the Trinity, God in Godself brings life and an altogether new—call it resurrected—reality. God in Godself has been resurrected. The Son is alive, the Father is given back his lost Son, and the Spirit is now thrust into the world, for from the Love of the Father and Son that has gone through death the Spirit looks to draw all death into the life of God so that death might be broken, and we and creation might be made new.

Easter is the proclamation in this world of death that the altogether new reality of God's future has dawned.[1] That God in Godself has been resurrected and overcomes death and now promises us that our deaths will die, that a new future beyond death is opened to us. It is a hope made possible by entering death, by entering and overcoming death with life—forevermore in Godself and soon to be for us too.

And this then is our ultimate hope, hope that comes through death. We hope as we trust that all our suffering, yearning, and brokenness has been taken by the Spirit and placed between the Love of the Father for the Son, a Love that is stronger than death by going through death. All those who despair can, in the power of the Spirit, take hope, for they are enveloped in the Love of Father and Son. Through their despair God is coming to them; in their despair God gives God's very person so that an altogether new reality might dawn from the future.

JESUS AS THE MAN OF THE FUTURE

Jesus Christ is this man of the future.[2] Just as now Jesus' humanity has been taken into God's future, we are promised that through his humanity our humanity too *will be* swept into God's future. This wholly new reality that we hope in is already, already right now; though it is in the future for us, it is *now* for Jesus. Jesus has borne the fullness of this reality, confronting and being overcome by the monster of death, only to overcome the monster with life through his death. Death can no longer touch Jesus, for after the Resurrection he is alive in God's future. He is unrecognizable to the men on the road to Emmaus and walks through walls (it seems) to encounter the disciples. Not because he is no longer human. Jesus is still human: "Touch my wounds," he invites Thomas, and calls out to the disciples to grill him a fish. No, he can do these things because he is living fully in God's future. He is now the human being of the future, promising us that through his broken and now alive humanity that we too will be resurrected with him, that we too will one day live fully in God's future (Rom. 14:8-9). We live next to death, but we hope, because he is alive, a new reality is on its way in which death is no more and love is the currency of all there is.

There is no salvation in death—only in life made possible by the Resurrection. But the Resurrection cannot be the Resurrection into God's future of new life unless it has borne the cross, unless it has taken fully annihilation into itself. The Resurrection is the dying of death because in the cross God absorbs death, making God's death the ground of an all-new life.[3] As Moltmann states, "Resurrection means 'life from the dead' (Rom. 9:15), and is itself connected with the annihilation of the power of death."[4] Hope is only hope next to death. We can only hope in this altogether new reality if we will, like our Lord, bear this one.[5] We must face death, for it is from within death that this altogether new reality is born. This new reality is in the future, but even now this new reality breaks into our world through the raw places of our brokenness, for it from brokenness that God encounters us, not simply providing encouragement, (this would be optimism), but offering God's very person as a new reality. *God forges this new reality of life and love through the material of our (and God's own) sorrow, yearning, loss, and brokenness.* Hope is hope through death. This is what makes it a secret.

It is through our despair that we encounter the God of hope. It is through our broken places that we find the resurrected Lord bringing a new reality from within this one. Hope springs from death, because our hope is in the man of the future, in Jesus Christ, who though he is overcome by death on the cross conquers death with life in the Resurrection. We must face death now; but if we face it we will discover with us the crucified and resurrected Jesus, who is our Lord, for he brings the reality of God's future. Now, though we are overwhelmed by loss, yearning, and brokenness, God seeks to bring life from these barren places. Though separation is our destiny, though we will be separated from those we love, from life itself, from our bodies, God promises, through God's own dead and made alive humanity in Jesus Christ, that no one will ever again be separated. It is when we feel most alone, isolated, and in despair that we can be sure that we are drawn into the life and Love of God, for this is where death exists after the cross and Resurrection. Even though death threatens us, it cannot determine our existence, for God has extracted its venom; God is bringing God's future. And when God's future reality comes in its fullness, death will be dismissed from existence. So we stand knee-deep in death and await and anticipate God's coming future.

THE CHURCH CARES ONLY FOR THE LIGHT AS IT LIVES IN DARKNESS

The church then has no real interest in death; the church is neither the community of optimism nor the cult of death.

The church has no interest in darkness; it seeks only the light, but light can only be found in darkness. To play flash-light light sabers with Owen, we first have to turn off the lights, placing ourselves in darkness not because we desire the darkness, but because it is only in being in the darkness that we are able to see the light. The problem with an opti-mistic church is that it spends all its energy on creating optimistic artificial light, seeking to pull people who know so well the darkness into faux light. An optimistic church seeks to cover the darkness. But the church of the cross seeks to make its life in what is, in darkness, hoping for the day when the darkness is no longer covered but is over-come completely by the dawn of God's future.

The church lives in the dark not because it worships darkness, but because it believes that by residing in dark-ness it encounters the brilliance and wonder of light. It believes that Jesus Christ is the light found in the dark, found next to our loss, yearning, and brokenness, giving us his humanity so that we might find new life beyond the darkness of death—this is our hope. Like the candle lit in the dark room, light's power is experienced in its shining in the dark, in its ability to spill into dark corners, exposing them, promising that a time is coming where the darkness of death will be swallowed by the dawn of a new reality. But until that day the church is the community that stands in the dark room, with a secret like a small candle, a secret that is powerful when we are reminded of the dark, a secret that the dawn is coming, that from the darkness of death will come life, that our wounds will be healed in the new reality of God's future.

FINDING MEANING WITHIN
THE DEATH OF MEANING

In a world where meaning has become so thin, as we saw in chapter 1, the church does the paradoxical: it seeks to construct meaning from within the void of meaning. It gives its people meaning by asking them to contemplate and practice the secret of God's future. We are given meaning not in this reality of death, but in bending our lives toward the altogether new reality of God's future that is on its way through death. Like crazy Minnesotans who bound from their houses with shorts, tank tops, and Frisbees upon the first forty-five-degree day of late March, so the church has meaning, as it does much the same. As it faces death, as it confronts a reality where the monster takes Benjamin and Denny, the church lives fully in this cold winter; yet nevertheless in the hope of the coming of summer, in the coming of God's future, it celebrates and anticipates what is not yet here but is on its way—new life through death. I was four years old when it first happened, when I first confronted head-on the monster of death; I spent many years hiding from its haunting as it felt like it was chasing me. I only wish someone, some community, in its words and life, would have embraced me, and in so doing that they would have turned my head toward death, calling me to face death and thereby discover that it was my Lord who encounters me. It is Godself who grabs me in the midst of my despair, giving me a promise that in my despair God will be present, and God promises a future where death is no more and friends are reunited and fathers and sons are safe, forevermore beyond death.

REFLECTING ON THE STORY OF SCRIPTURE

Peter and the Denial

Peter is an enigma. Peter is one of the first to confess that Jesus is the Christ. On their way to Jerusalem Jesus asked them flat out, "Who do you say that I am?" "You are the Christ," is Peter's response. But after affirming that he is right, Jesus explains that he must go and suffer and die, that the promise of salvation can only come from despair, just as

Isaac can only come from Sarah's barren womb and Israel become a people from their groaning of slavery. But of course Peter will have none of this dying part, telling Jesus he won't let it happen. In response to Peter's allergic reaction to death, Jesus rebukes Satan, addressing Peter as Satan—"Behind me, Satan," he says. The fear of death, the unwillingness to enter despair, is the root of great evil.

When Jesus is arrested, Peter is ready to serve death, to kill to keep himself from despair, from losing Jesus; but after cutting off a man's ear, Jesus stops him. Brave enough to follow, but not to own his association with Jesus, Peter denies him three times, watching as the night unfolds toward the utter despair of the death of God. But soon from the despair of the death of God comes the words that not even Peter can believe, the words that promise has sprouted from despair that God has overcome death in Jesus, that Jesus is alive.

Weeks later Jesus encounters Peter one last time on the beach. Jesus asks him, "Do you love me?" Of course Peter does, and he answers in the affirmative. But Jesus asks two more times, the three answers overcoming the three denials. Jesus' question is not, Do you believe in me? or Will you do my work? Jesus' question is, Do you love me? He is asking Peter if he will live from the love that enters death for the sake of life, if he will live for love that remains open to wounds and vulnerability. Do you love me? is the question. Will you suffer with me? Will you open your own suffering to me? After Peter's third answer Jesus tells him to then feed his sheep, to be a minister of the gospel out of the vulnerability of love, out of mutual despair bound in hope, rather than from power, organization, or knowledge. Jesus wants Peter to be the kind of minister of the gospel that loves, that enters despair, that is brave enough to admit his brokenness. Do you love? is the heart of ministry. Do we love? Are we brave enough to love by seeking God and one another through the promise of despair?

DISCUSSION QUESTIONS

- *What are your reactions to this text?*

- *Why is love more important for ministry than power, organization, or knowledge?*

- *What does it mean to have a secret that isn't about possessing information but is about a counter way of seeing existence?*

- *How would your congregation live out of this secret? How would you act to be a place that is more about hope than optimism?*

POSTSCRIPT

ANY WORK OF THIS KIND always leads the reader to ask the most important question, "What would this look like if a local church really tried to live out the ideas in these pages?" Sometimes this question is asked in skepticism, and sometimes in great appreciation, but in either case there is a desire to take what has been eye-opening and thought-provoking and place it within reach of our hands.

What I can offer is an invitation to look in on a community that is trying to do just this: seeking to take the theological and cultural ideas of this book and make them live in their context. Lake Nokomis Presbyterian Church is a small, urban church in Minneapolis that is endeavoring to enter into despair as the promise of God's presence. You're invited to watch as this small, in many ways insignificant, church seeks to be a community of love and hope in Jesus Christ born out of despair.

To look in, and even join the discussion, go to www.TheDespairProject.net. Here you'll find a description of this community, a blog on its journey, podcasts of sermons, and worship practices and liturgies that center on God's act and promise through despair.

NOTES

Introduction

1. Dietrich Bonhoeffer, *Ethics* (New York: Simon & Schuster, 1995), 83.
2. Walt Mueller, *Engaging the Soul of Youth Culture* (Downers Grove, Ill.: IVP, 2006), 58ff.
3. "Heidelberg Disputation" in *Luther's Works* (Philadelphia: Fortress Press, 1955), 31:52.

Part One

1. This move to assert that we now find ourselves beyond progress and in a time of nihilism of individual escape follows the work of David Lyon and his book *Postmodernity*. What should be understood is this assertion that we are in a time of nihilism is not a complete, airtight description, but rather what social theorists call an "ideal type." " 'Ideal types' are not descriptions of reality: they are the tools used to analyze it. . . . These tools are irreplaceable in any effort to fender thoughts intelligible and to enable a coherent narrative of the abominably messy evidence of human experience." Zygmunt Bauman, *Consuming Life* (Cambridge: Polity, 2007), 27.

1. Disneyland and the Defecating Goat

1. Richard Lane, *Jean Baudrillard* (London: Routledge, 2000), 95.
2. "This is the hyperreal—the more real than real." Chris Horrocks, *Introducing Baudrillard* (Cambridge: Icon Books, 1996), 109.
3. David Lyon, *Postmodernity* (Minneapolis: University of Minnesota Press, 1999), 21.

2. Life Is Like a Plastic Cup to Be Used and Disposed Of

1. Whereas in the last chapter I leaned heavily on Jean Baudrillard, in this chapter I will be drawing on the work of Anthony Giddens. Giddens and Baudrillard are not completely congruent dialogue partners. Giddens finds much in Baudrillard to be overstated. But while these

two giants of social theory are not easily fused, I believe there is enough overlap to justify mobilizing them for my purposes. Both do see great transitions and effects in a world that has moved beyond tradition, which is essential for this chapter.

2. Zygmunt Bauman, *Liquid Modernity* (Cambridge: Polity Press, 2000), 110.

3. "In modernity, tradition does not disappear; it is forced to explain itself. Modernity involves not the disappearance of tradition but its critical reinterpretation." Gerard Delanty, *Social Theory in a Changing World* (Cambridge: Polity Press, 1999), 167.

4. Anthony Giddens, *The Consequences of Modernity* (Stanford, Calif.: Stanford University Press, 1990), 40.

5. For more on this see Anthony Giddens and Christopher Pierson, *Conversations with Anthony Giddens: Making Sense of Modernity* (Stanford, Calif.: Stanford University Press, 1998), 133.

3. The Attack of the Zombies

1. This chapter theoretically is built on the groundwork Giddens helped lay in the last chapter on the loss of tradition. From this ground I have used Ulrich Beck and Zymunt Bauman to construct the ideas of this chapter (see Beck's *Risk Society* [London: Sage, 1992] and Bauman's *Liquid Modernity* [Cambridge: Polity Press, 2000]).

2. "The idea of 'risk society' might suggest a world which has become more hazardous, but this is not necessarily so. Rather, it is a society increasingly preoccupied with the future (and also with safety), which generates the notion of risk. . . . Essentially, 'risk' always has a negative connotation, since it refers to the chance of avoiding an unwanted outcome. But it can quite often be seen in a positive light, in terms of the taking of bold initiatives in the face of a problematic future. Successful risk-takers, whether in exploration, in business or in mountaineering, are widely admired." Anthony Giddens and Christopher Pierson, *Conversations with Anthony Giddens: Making Sense of Modernity* (Standford, Calif.: Standford University Press, 1998), 209.

3. "In an interview given to Jonathan Rutherford on 3 February 1999, Ulrich Beck . . . speaks of 'zombie categories' and 'zombie institutions' which are 'dead and still alive.' He names the family, class and neighbourhood as the foremost examples of that new phenomenon." Bauman, *Liquid Modernity*, 6.

4. Gerard Delanty, *Modernity and Postmodernity* (London: Sage, 2000), 122. He continues now following the thesis of Michel Maffesoli: "Unlike the communities of the past, which were spatial and fixed, emotional community is unstable and open, a product of the

fragmentation of the social and the disintegration of mass culture. People are increasingly finding themselves in temporary networks, or 'tribes,' organized around lifestyles and images." Ibid., 124.

5. Bauman asserts something similar following Hobsbawn: "As Eric Hobsbawm recently observed, 'never was the word "community" used more indiscriminately and emptily than in the decades when communities in the sociological sense became hard to find in real life'; and he commented, 'Men and women look for groups to which they can belong, certainly and forever, in a world in which all else is moving and shifting, in which nothing else is certain.'" Zygmunt Bauman, *Community: Seeking Safety in an Insecure World* (Cambridge: Polity, 2001), 15.

4. Hello! I'm My Body

1. In many ways this chapter brings the theoretical terrain of part one full circle. The preceding chapters have sought to deal with Baudrillard as well as Giddens and from him Beck and Bauman. In this chapter conversation about the need to formulate identity is borne within the work of Giddens, but as the chapter continues we will see how consumerism plays into this need for identity. Here we will be moving from the ground Giddens has laid to Bauman. Bauman, in his conversation on consumption, will lead us right back to Baudrillard.

2. "According to the latest calculation, a young American with a moderate level of education expects to change jobs at least eleven times during his or her working life—and the pace and frequency of change are almost certain to go on growing before the working life of the present generation is over. 'Flexibility' is the slogan of the day, and when applied to the labour market it augurs an end to the 'job as we know it,' announcing instead the advent of work on short-term contracts, rolling contracts or no contracts, positions with no in-built security but with the 'until further notice' clause. Working life is saturated with uncertainty." Zygmunt Bauman, *Liquid Modernity* (Cambridge: Polity Press, 2000), 147.

3. Tim Dant discusses how Baudrillard connects identity and body with the split between sign and signified. "[Baudrillard] distinguishes between the traditional symbolic significance of tattooing and costume, in which the body is something that is disguised with signs, and the modern fashion system, in which clothing, adornment and makeup are inscribed on the body in a signifying system whose dynamic is sexuality." Tim Dant, *Critical Social Theory* (London: Sage, 2003), 101.

4. David Lyon, *Postmodernity* (Minneapolis: University of Minnesota Press, 1999), 11.

Part Two

1. "This is not despair that a believer brings about oneself, but is rather itself evidence of God's workings. It is this despair that Luther encompasses in his term *Anfechtung*, and believed to be necessary before one appreciates and lives out a theology of the cross." Anna M. Madsen, *The Theology of the Cross in Historical Perspective* (Eugene, Oreg.: Pickwick Publications, 2007), 109.
2. Hall states helpfully, following Kierkegaard, "Existence, for Kierkegaard, was participation in despair and contradiction; and the only route to God across the 'yawning qualitative abyss' here that separates the divine from the human was the one that exists as God's possibility, namely, God's own willing entry into the impossibility and absurdity of our condition." Douglas John Hall, *Lighten Our Darkness: Toward an Indigenous Theology of the Cross* (Lima, Ohio: Academic Renewal Press, 2001), 123.
3. Gerhard Forde, in his very helpful book *On Being a Theologian of the Cross*, seeks to draw a distinction between "utter despair" and "ultimate despair," believing one is the despair of one's works and the other is the despair of impossibility. I simply don't find his distinction helpful. It feels like an easy distinction that can exist only in theory and not in practicality. It is a perspective that continues to contend that people are caught up in good works, rather than the despair that nothing works. "The 'utter despair of one's own ability' of thesis 18 is not the 'ultimate despair' of one still caught in the trap of presumption, but rather a despair that is preparation to receive the grace of Christ." Gerhard Forde, *On Being a Theologian of the Cross: Reflections on Luther's Heidelberg Disputation, 1518* (Grand Rapids, Mich.: Eerdmans, 1997), 66.
4. Hall, *Lighten Our Darkness*, 116.
5. This is the very point of Eberhard Jungel, who will be a major dialogue partner in the coming chapters.
6. "There is more to life as a follower of Jesus now than the *Anfechtungen*. There is plenty of scope for joy and thanksgiving and delight in the good things of creation. Luther took time to sniff a flower in the midst of his intense debate with the Catholic theologian Johann Eck. He delighted in his marriage to his Katie and spoke frequently about how wonderful it was to play with the children. But he insisted that a realistic assessment of life is called for if we are not to be wrong-footed by the devil when suffering inevitably comes." Mark Thompson, "Luther

on Despair," in Brian S. Rosner, ed., *The Consolations of Theology* (Grand Rapids, Mich.: Eerdmans, 2008), 67.

5. Will Death Ever Fall in Love?

1. This is Moltmann's very point. He works out the issue of theodicy around this theological commitment of a God who honors relationships—a God who is relational. I simply don't have the room to enter the thin air of theodicy here.
2. Eberhard Jungel, *God as the Mystery of the World* (Grand Rapids, Mich.; Eerdmans, 1983), 222.
3. "What Paul means when he asserts that he is determined to know and to preach only the one thing, 'Jesus Christ, and him crucified,' is that for him this represents the foundation and core of the whole Christian profession of belief. That is to say, he intends to consider every subject from the perspective that one acquires upon it when it is considered from the vantage point of the cross." Douglas John Hall, *Professing the Faith* (Minneapolis: Fortress Press, 1993), 364.
4. "For Luther, Christian thinking about God comes to an abrupt halt at the foot of the cross. The Christian is forced, by the very existence of the crucified Christ, to make a momentous decision. Either he will seek God elsewhere, or he will make the cross itself the foundation and criterion of his thought about God. The 'crucified God'—to use Luther's daring phrase—is not merely the foundation of the Christian faith, but is also the key to a proper understanding of the nature of God." Alister E. McGrath, *Luther's Theology of the Cross* (Malden, Mass.: Blackwell Publishing, 1985), 1.
5. Jungel beautifully drives this point deeper: "For Paul, the Crucified One is weak, subject to death. But Paul does not celebrate this thought with melancholy, but rather thinks of it as the gospel, as a source of joy. What is joyful about the weakness of the Crucified One? The weakness of the Crucified One is for Paul the way in which God's power of life is perfected (2 Cor. 13:4). Weakness is then not understood as a contradiction of God's power. There is, however, only one phenomenon in which power and weakness do not contradict each other, in which rather power can perfect itself as weakness. This phenomenon is the event of love. Love does not see power and weakness as alternatives." Jungel, *God as the Mystery of the World*, 206.
6. Moltmann states, "To understand what happened between Jesus and his God and Father on the cross, it is necessary to talk in Trinitarian terms. The Son suffers dying, the Father suffers the death of the Son. The grief of the Father here is just as important as the death of the Son. The Fatherlessness of the Son is matched by the Sonlessness of the

157

Father, and if God has constituted himself as the Father of Jesus Christ, then he also suffers the death of his Fatherhood in the death of the Son." *The Crucified God* (Minneapolis: Fortress Press, 1974), 243.

7. "But how can the death of Jesus on the cross be understood as God's action, even as God's suffering? Paul goes even one step further in II Cor. 5.19ff., when he says 'God was in Christ.' In other words, God not only acted in the crucifixion of Jesus or sorrowfully allowed it to happen, but was himself active with his own being in the dying Jesus and suffered with him. If God has reconciled the world to himself through the cross, then this means that he has made himself visible in the cross of Christ and, as it were, says to man, 'Here I am!'" Ibid., 190.

8. Moltmann says it like this, "God has made this death part of his life, which is called love and reconciliation. 'God himself is dead,' as it is said in a Lutheran hymn; the consciousness of this fact expresses the truth that the human, the finite, frailty, weakness, the negative, is itself a divine moment, is in God Himself." Ibid., 254.

9. Moltmann says, "God and suffering are no longer contradictions . . . but God's being is in suffering and the suffering is in God's being itself, because God is love." Ibid., 227.

10. Jungel drives this point deeper than I have space to do: "It is only short-circuited criticism which wants to see here a final triumph of death. Rather, what happens here is that turning around of death into life which is the very essence of love. . . . Death is not turned around apart from love, because love alone is able to involve itself in the complete harshness of death." Jungel, *God as the Mystery of the World*, 364.

11. J. B. Webster, *Eberhard Jungel: An Introduction to His Theology* (London: Cambridge, 1986), 85.

6. This Is No Pep Rally; This Is an Actuality

1. "Luther was not at all interested in escaping suffering, but rather in running toward it. In this way suffering was not to be understood as means to an end, namely something to be overcome in order to reach God, but rather itself was evidence of God reaching toward humanity, abiding with it in the midst of the world's sorrows. Luther advanced thereby an 'earthy' God, one who mingles and remains with the despairing and the abandoned." Anna M. Madsen, *The Theology of the Cross in Historical Perspective* (Eugene, Oreg.: Pickwick Publications, 2007), 87-88.

2. "Paul says in even stronger terms: 'He made him sin for us' (II Cor. 5.21) and 'He became a curse for us' (Gal. 3.13). Thus in the total, inextricable abandonment of Jesus by his God and Father, Paul sees the delivering up of the Son by the Father for godless and

godforsaken man." Jürgen Moltmann, *The Crucified God* (Minneapolis: Fortress Press, 1974), 242.

3. Douglas John Hall says something very similar when he states, "The question therefore becomes: How can one at the same time acquire sufficient honesty about what needs to be faced, and sufficient hope that facing it would make a difference. To engage in altering the course of our present world towards life and not death?" Hall, *God and Human Suffering: An Exercise in the Theology of the Cross* (Minneapolis: Fortress Press, 1986), 47.

4. Moltmann, *The Crucified God*, 1.

5. Ibid., 19, 18.

7. A Funeral for the Trinity

1. Jungel shows the biblical roots of this perspective: "As we have seen from our examination of the Old Testament, death means relationlessness. As the wages of sin, a view which we find more in the New Testament, death is the consequence of man's pernicious drive toward this relationlessness. Man's disastrous urge toward the deadliness of relationlessness stands in direct proportion to death's aggressiveness as alienating man from God and as breaking up human relationships. Now while in the Old Testament God is understood as standing at an infinite distance from death, wholly untouched by the deadliness of relationlessness, in the death of Jesus he endures contact with death. By identifying himself with the dead Jesus, God truly exposed himself to the alienating power of death. He exposed his own divinity to the power of negation. And he did precisely this in order to be God for all men." Eberhard Jungel, *Death: The Riddle and the Mystery* (Philadelphia: Westminster Press, 1974), 109.

2. Jürgen Moltmann says it like this: "God does not become a religion, so that man participates in him by corresponding religious thoughts and feelings. God does not become a law, so that man participates in him through obedience to a law. God does not become an ideal, so that man achieves community with him through constant striving. He humbles himself and takes upon himself the eternal death of the godless and the godforsaken, so that all the godless and godforsaken can experience communion with him." Jürgen Moltmann, *The Crucified God* (Minneapolis: Fortress Press, 1974), 276.

8. Does Death Wear a Helmet?

1. This is the very argument of twentieth-century Italian Marxist Antonio Gramsci.

2. Douglas John Hall states, "A theology which looks to God's solidarity with the broken creation and aims to participate in God's healing of that creation *must* involve itself in the specifics of its society's problematique, including its economics, its foreign policies, its long- and short-range goals." Douglas John Hall, *Thinking the Faith* (Minneapolis: Fortress Press, 1991), 39.

3. Hall says it this way: "God in Christ absorbs the negating consequences of injustice, unpeace, and the disintegration of the creation. God does not cancel out these realities, but creates new conditions under which they may come to serve God's creational intentions." Douglas John Hall, *Professing the Faith* (Minneapolis: Fortress Press, 1996), 313.

4. Anna Madsen states, "Paul repeatedly emphasizes participation in Jesus' death which begins with the believer's baptism into his death. That participation necessarily means working with and for other Christians, particularly those suffering weakness or poverty." Anna M. Madsen, *The Theology of the Cross in Historical Perspective* (Eugene, Oreg.: Pickwick Publications, 2007), 56.

9. Christian Faith Is a Secret That Must Be Kept

1. Jürgen Moltmann says it this way: "Easter was a prelude to, and a real anticipation of, God's qualitatively new future and the new creation in the midst of the history of the world's suffering." Jürgen Moltmann, *The Crucified God* (Minneapolis: Fortress Press, 1974), 163.

2. "In that one man the future of the new world of life has already gained power over this unredeemed world of death and has condemned it to become a world that passes away. Therefore, in faith in the risen Jesus, men already live in the midst of the transitory world of death from the powers of the new world of life that have dawned in him." Ibid., 171.

3. Eberhard Jungel says it this way: "Resurrection means the overcoming of death. But death will cease to be only when it no longer consumes the life which excludes it, but when life has absorbed death into itself." Eberhard Jungel, *God as the Mystery of the World* (Grand Rapids, Mich.: Eerdmans, 1983), 364.

4. Moltmann, *The Crucified God*, 170.

5. Anna Madsen helpfully places these ideas within Pauline theology: "It appears, then, that although Paul places great weight upon the cross, he wishes his readers to keep the resurrection always in mind, as it is only the two together that reflect God's complete action on behalf of God's creation." Anna M. Madsen, *The Theology of the Cross in Historical Perspective* (Eugene, Oreg.: Pickwick Publications, 2007), 22.

INDEX